A Daughter of the State

by Kathleen Dalley

To my dear friends Geoff and Jackie
Barker

QueenSpark Book 32

Published by QueenSpark Books, Brighton
First Edition, March 1998

Book production by Jackie Blackwell, Michelle White,
Stephanie Cole, Jane Carlisle, Anne-Fay Townsend.

QueenSpark Books are grateful to Brighton & Hove
Libraries for the use of the cover photograph.

ISBN 0 904733 61 0

Printed by Digaprint Ltd., Brighton, Sussex

Foreword

Save the Children believes in a world where discrimination against children has no place, where children are valued as equal members of society with an important contribution to make and where childhood is recognised and respected as a crucial period in everyone's life. We champion the right to a happy, healthy and secure childhood.

Volunteers are essential to fundraising in the UK particularly in shops which are staffed entirely by volunteers. We are especially grateful to Miss Dalley and to all the other volunteers at the Hove shop for their commitment and hard work raising funds in support of the Fund's aims working for a better world for children.

working for a better world for children
Save the Children Y

PART ONE

Babyhood

One to be ready, two to be steady, and three to be off.

It was a beautiful spring day in 1922, the sky was blue, the sun was shining and we children were so very happy running races in a lovely garden. Nurse Saunders was playing races with us. We raced up the drive to the closed gate and then back to Nurse Saunders who was sitting on a circular wooden seat that surrounded the horse-chestnut tree. We were having such fun. If one of the others stayed with us they usually just sat and darned socks, but Nurse Saunders was different.

We were residents at the Receiving Home in Hornsey Rise, Islington; a group of three to five year olds who would spend most afternoons, if weather permitted, playing in this garden. Altogether there were about thirty children in the home, aged from birth to five years and most, like me, had been at the home since we were born. Some were foundlings, some had been abandoned or lost parents through accidents and one or two were there while parents were in hospital, or going through difficult times.

On this glorious day, we were so busy playing that we did not notice a green van, with people inside, coming up the drive. When we stopped playing we saw that there were some ladies watching us. They were all dressed alike in long butchers blue striped dresses with high neck bands. Little white caps rested on their heads, all round and gathered and so flat they looked like plates. They had come from St John's Workhouse and we were told that these ladies were our mothers. Nurse Saunders took me to my mother. I can remember that I did not want to stay with her, but Nurse Saunders said,

'You must stay, it is only for a little while.'

My mother took me to the circular seat and shortly the other children and their mothers came to join us. She sat me on her lap and gave me some sweets. She told me that I would soon be five years old and then I would be taken away from the Receiving Home. I would instead live in a very big house and start school. This was all very puzzling and I did not really understand what she was telling me. I had so many questions to ask and firstly said,

'What is a mother?' and 'Why do you wear that funny hat?'
But she was unable to answer as suddenly a whistle was blown and she, along with the other ladies in their funny clothes, got up and went straight back to the green van. They got inside and were driven away. After it had left, we ran back to kindly Nurse Saunders, who we all loved. We had so many questions to ask her about 'mothers' and 'schools'and later that evening we asked Nurse Saunders our questions. Usually, when she put us to bed she would tell us stories, but this night she tried to answer our questions.

'School,' she said, 'is a place where you learn to read and write.'

'Will we come back here?'

'No, never, we only have babies here and you will all be big children.'

'What is a mother?'

'She is somebody that loves you.'

'Do you mean like Jesus loves us?'

'No, not quite that, she is somebody that brought you here to us.'

'Was she wearing those funny clothes?'

'Yes, I think so. You see, your mother was in St John's Road Workhouse when you were born and she could not keep you with her, so she brought you here."

Minnie Ha Ha asked,

'Why didn't my mother come and see me?" .

'Because you haven't got one. You came to us by chance.'

Minnie did not understand and neither did we, but we accepted it. Then we said our prayers as we did every night.

Jesus tender shepherd hear me
Bless thy little lambs tonight
Through the darkness be thou near me
Keep me safe till morning light

When we were ready for sleep, Minnie Ha Ha (she was called this because she was always laughing), sat up in bed and said that she did not want to go to school. We all got up and agreed with her. Maud, who was a tomboy, climbed out of her cot and took our cot sides down so that we could join her. It was fun. We had a game of hide and seek, we hid under the babies' cots and pushed up the springs with our backs so we woke them all up. Then we climbed up to the barred windows and sat on the window sill to watch the buses go by and wave to the people outside. The babies yelling and our laughter soon brought Nurse Saunders and Officer Hassell upstairs. Officer Hassell was very strict and would have slapped each one of us if Nurse Saunders had not been with her. When we were eventually back in our cots, Nurse Saunders stayed with us for a while and did some mending. She assured us that school was a lovely place. She said that Ada and I both had sisters there and that Maud had a brother. But as adults seldom chatted to us we had little knowledge, so brothers and sisters, mothers and school actually meant very little to us.

While we lived at the Receiving Home our routine was practically the same every day. After we had been woken in the morning, we went into the dining room for breakfast. When we had eaten our tripe and drunk the milk diluted with hot water, we spent the rest of the morning in the Playroom, left entirely on our own, until dinner time. The Playroom was a large empty room with a couple of forms by the walls and two or three baby chairs hanging from the ceiling. There was always a baby screaming and we toddlers were expected to push them to keep them quiet. There was nothing much for us to do except fight with one another for a place in front of the window or tease the babies, but mostly we sat down by the wall miserably waiting for dinner. The Officers always seemed too busy to play as there were babies to bath and bottle feed, beds to make and general chores to do. Dinner was the same every day, minced meat, potatoes and rice pudding and for tea we would just have bread and margarine with diluted milk to drink. After a rest in the afternoon we played in the garden if weather permitted. There was always somebody with us, usually an Officer who just sat and did mending or knitting. It was only Nurse Saunders who would play games with us, but that did not happen very often.

Sundays were lovely days. A lady used to come in from the church at the bottom of Crouch End Hill. She used to play the celesta and teach us songs about Jesus and sometimes she would give us little pictures from the Bible stories. On Sunday afternoons we would put on little red capes and go out for a walk. We must have looked a sight. The two Officers would push the prams that had about three or four babies in them and we toddlers walked in crocodile fashion. We loved to run down Crouch End Hill when we could get away from the line and the Officers.

Some time after my mother's visit, the green van arrived again but this time nobody came out of it, except the driver. Standing waiting in the hall there were six of us little ones, Charlie, Thomas, Maud, Minnie, Ada and myself, all washed and dressed with our capes on. Nurse Saunders took us outside and put us in the back of the van then got in with us, closing the back door. We had nothing of our own, not even a toy between us so there were no packing cases. The van was rather dark as the only window was on the door. We sat on long wooden stools, one on each side of the van. We were on our way to the big Children's Home and School.

Our babyhood had ended.

St Mary's, School and Vaccination

We had never been in a vehicle before, so it should have been a lovely adventure. But the van went very fast, the stools slid about and it had a nasty smell of oil and so we arrived at St Mary's in a very miserable state.

On arrival, the drive looked very pleasant. On the right there was an assortment of trees, a red horse-chestnut and some copper beech amongst others. They almost hid the large wall topped with broken pieces of glass. This wall surrounded all of the buildings. To the left and over the privet hedge there was the boys' playground marked out for football. Next to this was the Master and Matron's house. It looked very grand to us children. It was built in its own grounds encircled by a lovely garden. When the front door opened you could see a beautiful staircase with a red carpet and brass rods. I was never to go in the front of the house, but I do know that there was a staircase that led to the first floor of the boys, girls and infants' dormitories. At the back of the house was a passage that led into the children's Dining Hall. Further along the corridor was the detention room. This room was empty apart from a small table, chair, stool and two canes that hung on the door. I was to be sent there several times for some misdemeanour, to stand outside this room, but I was never taken in or given the cane. This does not mean that I was never punished and the fear of being caned was always there.

Further down the drive was the girls' playground, a large empty area surrounded by the broken glass topped wall. On the left was the infants' house, a very square building, similar to the girls' house, only smaller. Past the infants' house was the tennis court. This was mostly used by Matron and her visitors and just now and again by members of staff. At the end of the drive was the Sick Bay. Most of the buildings looked severe and ugly. I'm sure that they could not have been built for children. On some of the window sills there were filled-in holes as though there had been bars up at the windows. Perhaps it had been a prison or a remand home before.

Charlie had been very sick in the van and Nurse Saunders took him on her lap and tried to comfort him. Once we stopped we were taken from the van directly to the Sick Bay. From the outside the Sick Bay looked like a comfortable double-fronted house with bay windows. There were balconies with access from the upper floor windows and a large green front door with brass fittings. The front step was hearthstoned. This entrance was used only by the Matron and the Doctor; staff and children used the back door. Inside the Sick Bay there was a very bright hallway with highly polished fixed benches on each side. A picture of the Chairman of the Board of Guardians hung on the wall. Through the hallway was a very dark passage dimly lit by a faint gas light. It had a stone floor with brown walls and on each side were the wards. At the rear of the Sick Bay was an alleyway facing the very high glass topped wall, which led round to the front of the building. On one side were stacks of coal and on the other was a rubbish pit, where the rubbish from all departments was thrown. A horse with dust cart came over once a week to clear it up, but there was always a nasty smell. It was one that we got used to. The lane in front of the Sick Bay opened onto a cobbled road. On the left of the road were the noisy, hissing laundry and boiler houses and on the right was a square building; the girls' house. You could still see the wall above these buildings.

We were taken through the back entrance of the Sick Bay, straight to the receiving room. Even when a child was very ill, it was always taken round the back of the house. The Receiving Room was very big with light green walls and dark green doors. Under our feet was a stone cold floor and we waited quietly while the Officers chatted to Nurse Saunders who was giving them our particulars. Eventually the two boys were taken into another room and we were stripped and left standing naked. The clothes that we had been wearing were folded, checked and signed for by Nurse Saunders. Next she went into the room with the boys. We heard her saying goodbye to them and telling the Officer that Charlie was not very strong, and that he was poorly at times. The Officer replied,

'Oh, don't worry, he will survive, most of them do.'

She came in to us girls and kissed us all, saying,

'Be good, I will try and come and see you when I bring more children along.'

Then she left, leaving us six sobbing naked little ones.

Shortly afterwards another Nurse came in, a very cheerful buxom lady. She sang while she attended to us and told us that she had come from a land far away called Wales. First of all she examined our heads and then took us to the bathroom where the boys had been; we were weighed and had a lovely hot bath. At last we were brought in some clothes; we had been left naked for what appeared to us a very long time. The clothes were awful; a flannel vest, a liberty bodice with lots of buttons, a pair of knickers and a navy blue serge dress with buttons down the back. The vest and dress were very itchy, although we did get used to them. There were black woolly socks and black lace-up boots, which took ages to get fitted with. Previously we had never worn clothes that needed buttoning or lacing. I expect that they chose simple styles at the Receiving Home so that we could dress ourselves.

When we had been fitted with our clothes we were taken to the wards in the Sick Bay; the boys in one and we girls next door. We could see the boys through a glass partition. There were four beds in each ward with white counterpanes that made the wards look brighter. There was very little furniture, just a table and chairs in the middle and a basket under each bed to put your clothes in. A Nurse brought each of us a slice of bread and margarine and a mug of tea but we were so unhappy that none of us ate or drank anything. Shortly after this we were put to bed and we settled down very quickly, crying ourselves to sleep.

The next morning we were not allowed to get dressed as Dr Jenkins was coming to see us, so our first breakfast of porridge was taken at the table in the ward. The Doctor went to see the boys first. We could hear him laughing and we thought him very nice. When he came in to see us he had a sheepdog with him, called Peter. The dog was very big with a thick woolly coat and he loved being patted. When the Doctor left, Nurse said we were still not to get dressed as we were going to be vaccinated. The boys were taken to the receiving room first. All was quiet for a while and then there were the most awful screams. When we heard Charlie cry we did not worry too much, but with Thomas it was different as he very seldom cried. We looked through the partition when the boys came back to their ward. They were still crying, and we saw that Thomas had a bandage on his arm. We girls huddled together and were so very frightened that at first we refused to go with the Nurse when she came to fetch us. Despite our protests we were taken back to the Receiving Room where we had been the day before. It was sparsely furnished with a weighing machine, a dentist's chair, two wooden chairs and a small table that Doctor Jenkins sat at. On the table were two enamel trays with lots of bits and pieces on them. Dr Jenkins told Nurse to put Maud on her lap and to hold her arm still. Nurse Lloyd took hold of Maud, squeezed her closely to her breasts, and said,

'Sit still, this won't hurt.'

The word "hurt" was enough to warn us that whatever it was, it *was* going to hurt. We three, still in our night-dresses with bare feet, stood watching. Suddenly there was pandemonium. Maud screamed, the tray went flying, Doctor's glasses fell off and Maud ran back to the ward. Nurse Lloyd, with her cap all askew and the bib of her apron torn, chased after her. We heard her slap Maud very hard and she was brought back screaming to the room and strapped into the dentist chair.

I was the next one to be vaccinated. I was too scared to cry. I think that my fear was greater than the pain as Dr Jenkins scratched away at a few places on my left arm. I had to wait for the others to be vaccinated. When it came to Maud's turn again, Doctor asked if she was going to be a good girl, and did she want to be vaccinated strapped in the chair, or sitting on Nurse Lloyd's lap? Maud replied that she did not want anything and she told Doctor that he was very naughty to hurt her arm and that she would tell Nurse Saunders. In the end Maud was vaccinated while she was still in the dental chair. She didn't cry then, but we all cried when we got back into the ward. It was a very traumatic experience for us all and for a very long time afterwards, I was afraid of any change and was scared of meeting new people.

We stayed in the Sick Bay for a few days where our arms were looked at and dressed by Nurse Lloyd every day. Then we were transferred to Maxwell House, the infants' house, which was to be our home for the next two years.

On our arrival at Maxwell House, we were introduced to Officer Jackson. Nurse Lloyd told her that we were all from Hornsey Rise Receiving Home and she said that, *as usual*, we had been spoilt by Nurse Saunders. Soon after, a lot of children came running into the playroom, immediately took off their coats, hung them up and put on pinafores. Then they went straight into the washrooms to get ready for dinner. Suddenly a bell began to ring and immediately the children stood in line. We were told by a big girl that this was where we stood every time the first bell rang. Then a second bell rang and the big girl, called Angela, took hold of my hand and we marched into the Dining Hall. This was a huge hall situated on the ground floor of the main building which seated approximately three hundred children. On the right side sat the girls, with the boys on the left and the infants in the middle. At the front of the hall was a platform where the Band boys played as we marched into meals. Also on the platform was the bell rope. We would be stood under this rope if we wet the bed or were naughty. This bell would summon us into all our meals. Next to it was the pulpit used on Sundays by the Vicar and at other times by the Master who would lecture us on our misdemeanours. At the other end of the hall were the hot plates and the door into the kitchens. Through the kitchens were the boys' house and drill yard.

The boys' house was a square building, with dormitories on two floors. At the back of the boys quarters there was an alleyway that led into the Tailor and Shoe shops and Band room. As always, the glass-topped wall could still be seen above these buildings. Beyond this were the Visiting Room and Lodge. Behind the Lodge was the top of the very long drive which led to the large brown spike-topped gates that we entered on our first day in July 1922.

The Band was playing and it did not stop until the great hall was full of children all standing in their places ready for dinner. After grace was said the senior children formed a line in front of the hot plates.

The Officers served the food under the beady eye of Mr. Jacobs, the Headmaster. Plates were passed along the line to each table, we infants being served first. Only then could we sit down and eat our meal. We were not allowed to put our elbows or arms on the table. Talking was not allowed at dinner time or breakfast, but it was allowed during tea.

After dinner the other children returned to school and we six were escorted by Officer Jackson to the Tailor shop to be fitted with heavy navy blue school coats. After this we were taken to school to see the Headmistress, Miss Pugh. When we arrived in the Assembly Hall some other children were there with their mothers. Officer Jackson sat on a chair among the mothers and we sat on the floor. When Miss Pugh came into the hall, she asked us children to stand up, and said that we were to do this each time she came into our classroom. She came and chatted to us all together and then individually; she seemed a very kindly person. She asked Officer Jackson if we were all five years old because we were so much smaller than the other children. Also, she hoped that we would be able to tie up our boot laces before we came to school after the summer holidays. We were then shown to the classrooms; Minnie, Thomas and me with four other children in one, and Maud, Ada and Charlie, in the other. We now had something to look forward to.

Life at St Mary's and School

For the next two years we led a life of strict discipline and instant obedience. Life was, at first, a bit hard. We had to learn that rules and routine came before anything else at St Mary's and the only day that we had any play was Saturday. We were ruled mainly by the bell hung in the dining hall and when that rope was pulled everybody jumped to it. The first bell was pulled by the fat slovenly Night Officer. She would come round the dormitories and throw open the windows, whatever the weather, and we would all get up. When we were dressed we went to the end of the room and sat on the floor until the senior girls had finished making our beds. Then they took us downstairs and we washed and combed our hair to get ready for breakfast. When the bell went again we stood in line in our seating order. At the sound of the next bell we marched to the music of the band into the dining hall. Breakfast was already served so we were able to sit down and eat it but only after Grace had been said. When we had finished our breakfast the Senior Officer in charge would say prayers and then we would sing a hymn. We would march again to the band, but this time out of the dining hall. We would never walk in or out of that room. Then we had to hurry to tidy ourselves up, put on our hats and coats, and stand in line until the bell rang for us to go to school. So it went on like this throughout the day and all the other days that I spent at St Mary's.

After we had been at Maxwell House for about a fortnight or so, the red plasters were removed from our arms as they were now better and an incredible thing happened to the whole of St Mary's. We were taken away to Dover Court Bay on a camping holiday for two weeks.

At Dover Court Bay we stayed in a big camp of corrugated sheds and we slept on mattresses on the ground. We had no sheets, just blankets that were itchy and not very comfortable. But it was great fun as the usual discipline went out the window. We did not have to put our boots on in the morning but ran about in our bare feet. We went to the beach on most days usually to paddle and run about, but we never did swim.

It was while we were on this wonderful holiday that I first met my sister Eva; she was twelve years old then. We were sitting at breakfast on the first morning and there was no senior girl to serve us our porridge. Instead Officer Bishop sent over someone we had not met before, a tall, graceful girl, with long wavy brown hair. Officer Bishop told her each of our names and when she came to me said,

'this is your sister.'

Eva was very pretty with chestnut coloured hair and hazel eyes. She had a cheerful disposition and seemed popular with the other girls and well liked by the staff. Eva smiled and came straight over to me and said,

'Isn't she lovely and so little!'

Officer Bishop seemed most annoyed and said,

'She has been spoiled enough already and if you are going to be of any help to me you are to treat all the children alike.'

Eva did not appear to hear her and continued to talk to me. She told me that she would love and care for me and that she had always wanted a little sister. Despite Officer Bishop's concern about unfair treatment, she had no real worry however, as Eva appeared to love all of us.

Later that day with the help of two other girls, Eva took us all down to the beach to play. She took Ada, Jean, who was a little crippled girl, and me, paddling. It was the first time I had seen the sea, what a big bath it was! And when the water splashed wasn't it salty! Eva told us to walk in her footsteps and we had such confidence in my sister that we obeyed. When the water became too deep Eva picked up Jean and Ada and I followed them back to the beach.

We had many wonderful days at Dover Court Bay, but it was all over too soon and after two weeks we returned to the discipline and routine of St Mary's, and went back to school. If it had not been for the fact that we went to school and had this annual holiday, our lives would have been sheer hell.

School was a godsend to me, it was a wonderful place. I enjoyed every one of my days there. We children from St Mary's were usually the first to arrive in the school playground and it was so lovely to be able to run about, shout and play. There was a fixed rocking horse and a roundabout that we could climb on. We had a lot of fun in the few minutes before the whistle went for us to get into our lines and walk into school. After our teacher had called the register we walked in a quiet orderly fashion into the Hall for assembly. Here there was no-one to push or poke us because we were not expected to march or hold our heads up, everything was more congenial and relaxed.

At twelve o'clock we came out of school for dinner and were met by three senior girls; Eva, Sarah and Gladys. They took us back to Maxwell House and life was again a rush until we returned to school. The senior girls would often teach us dances during playtimes at school. They taught us to do the *Charleston* and the *Black Bottom*. Eva would tie tape around our foreheads and we would dance for the big girls; this was good fun. I was so tiny they would stand me up on a bench and get me to dance. I loved all the fuss and the big girls would give us sweets.

At 4 o'clock, when classes were finished, Officer Jackson would be waiting for us. We had to wait for Eva, Sarah and Gladys because there were too many of us for her to take back alone, but we didn't mind as it meant that we could have a bit more play. Back at St Mary's there were no toys or games and there was no time for any play when we got there. As soon as we got indoors and had hung up our hats and coats we had to sit down and wait on long forms in the playroom; girls on one side and boys on the other, while the senior children cleaned our boots. After tea, one round of bread and margarine with a mug of tea (no sugar), we all had to have our heads combed. Eva told me that my head looked the same every day but nobody had shown her or the other helpers what to look for. However, if she saw us scratching our heads she would send us to the Officer who treated hair with some horrible smelly stuff called sassafras. The smell was so horrible you could not go into the dining hall and so you went without tea. Once, when this happened to me, Eva stole some bread and brought a drink of water for me.

Every night at 6pm the first bed bell was rung for we infants to march upstairs to our dormitory. We were bathed every other night, but not on Sundays, alternating with the boys. We hated bath nights.

There were two baths in the bathroom, they were very high and you had to climb up three steps to get into them. There was an Officer at each bath. Three senior girls were there to help any of us and on the boys' night they had the help of senior boys. We had to leave our clothes and night-dresses in the dormitory and run into the bathroom naked. We would do the same in reverse after our baths. As we climbed into the bath, before we had time to sit down, we were soaped all over starting with our faces. Most of the soap went into our eyes and mouths. Then we were pushed into the sitting position, rinsed and lifted out. One night a week our hair was washed and we were pushed backwards for our hair to be rinsed. This was very frightening, but if we cried we were spanked. In fact, spanking was very frequent on bath nights. If we had done something wrong during the day, even if we had already been smacked for it, Officer Bishop would make a point of seeing that she bathed you. She took great delight in seeing how red she could make our bottoms and thighs, she really was a bully. The senior girls used to do their best to protect us and I think Eva must have got me out of many a scrape on bath nights.

Family

One morning after breakfast, when I was about six years old, Officer Jackson told me that I was not to get ready for school. Instead I was to wait in the playroom as my sister was coming to fetch me to take me out. When Eva came she was dressed in very different clothes and they looked most weird. She was wearing a badly creased brown frock which looked as though it had been rolled up for a very long time. It was buttoned from the waist to the neck, the buttons were all odd and the sleeves were too short. However, the ugly clothes did not mar Eva's looks. She had brushed out the plaits in her lovely hair and had tied it back with a bright yellow bow. The clothes that she had brought me to put on were all screwed up as well. There was a red flannel petticoat and a pale blue woolly frock which was very long, so Eva tied a piece of elastic round my waist to shorten it. We did keep our boots on though. As we walked alone up the drive to the Lodge gates, everything seemed very quiet and strange. Eva told me that when we got outside the gates Mother would be waiting for us and that she would be with Uncle Jack.

'He is the man that Mother is going to marry today.'

'Does that mean,' I asked, 'that we will have a father?'

'Nothing of the kind,' said Eva irritably, 'he will never be our father and you are to call him Uncle Jack. Do you understand?'

By this time we had got to the Lodge. Mr Ridgeway, the Lodgekeeper, opened the gate and asked Mother to step into the lodge. Mother also had different clothes. Instead of her long, dark blue uniform frock, she was wearing a green coat with a very large black hat that had brilliant bright red cherries on it. We watched Mother go to a desk and sign a book. She kissed and squeezed Eva and then me. I hated this because she always squeezed me too tightly. When we got outside the gate I met Uncle Jack, who was a very thin pale-faced man. His hair was fair and closely shaved to the head and he was smoking a white clay pipe. He patted me on the head and said,

'I will soon be your daddy.'

Eva said,

'I have told her to call you Uncle Jack, and marriage or no marriage, that is what we will always call you.'

Mother took hold of my hand and was about to walk with me when Eva took me away from her. Eva told her to walk with Uncle Jack and said that we would follow them. We walked along Hornsey Road and passed our school. I wished I was going in but we continued up the road to Highbury, along Upper Street to Islington Town Hall. We joined a queue of people and stood for a very long time. Mother met some friends and talked with them. I got bored and began to wriggle because I wanted to go to the lavatory. Eva took me outside, round the back of the building where there were some trees and bushes and we both did a wee behind a tree. When we got back they were calling for Mother and Mr Jack Wells. We were ushered, along with Mother's friends, into a big room. It looked very dark because the walls had brown panelling and small windows that were close up to the ceiling. Eva and I were told to sit on a long form at the back of the room while Mother and Uncle Jack, with two friends, went to the front where there were two men sitting at a desk. They talked together for quite a long time and then I saw them sign a book. Eva stayed very quiet all this time and in fact hardly spoke for the rest of the day.

When we came out of the Town Hall with Mother's two friends, the man, whose name was Fred, said that he would treat us to dinner. We went to an Eel and Pie shop and as we went in, I noticed a big white enamel bowl full of large worms swimming in it. Mother said that they were eels which were very nice to eat and we would be having them for our dinner. I could not look at them, let alone eat them and when the cut-up pieces were put in front of me, Eva took them off my plate and onto her own. I just ate mashed potato with parsley sauce.

We left Mother's friends at the shop and we walked towards Caledonian Road. It was very busy with trams and carts going to and fro. We passed a big building of grey stone that looked like a castle. Eva said that it was a prison, a place where bad people go. After some time we arrived at a house with ever so many stairs and when we got to the top we were shown into a dark attic room. There was an argument between Mother and the landlady about rent or suchlike and we came all the way downstairs and left. We visited several more places and eventually settled for one in the basement of a very large house. I was so tired that I fell asleep before I was put to bed.

When I awoke the next morning I found that I had been put into a cot and felt very indignant as I had been sleeping in a bed for a long time. I looked through the bars and there was Eva, Mother and Uncle Jack, all asleep on a mattress on the floor. All of us were still wearing the clothes that we had on the day before. I climbed out of the cot and woke Eva up. She put her finger to my lips to be quiet, then we put on our boots and she took me outside in the yard where there was a lavatory with a broken door and a water tap. She splashed my face and hands with the cold water and dried me with the skirt of her white petticoat. When we got back inside, Mother and Uncle Jack were up and had packed our meagre belongings. Mother told us that she was taking us to see her sister, Ethel, in Holloway Road. We left the house and on our way to Holloway Road we stopped at a wayside café for a cup of tea and some buttered toast.

Auntie Ethel was a tall, thin lady; she looked very much like Eva with her lovely head of chestnut coloured hair worn in a plait around her head. The house was very warm and cosy. It had two rooms and a scullery downstairs and three bedrooms upstairs. The room over the scullery was very small. Auntie had five children, three boys and two girls, and she told Mother that she had got "one in the box" again. I was mystified and wondered where she kept the box. Perhaps she kept it in the parlour, I thought, but we were not taken in there.

Auntie Ethel made us all very welcome. We were taken to the kitchen where there was a big pot of stew on the stove and a kettle hissing away. Mother asked after Uncle Harry and Auntie replied that we had just missed him as he was on a late shift but would be back later that evening. Auntie took Eva's dress off her and ironed it and she went to find me a shorter dress and put a shawl round my shoulders. Then we all sat around the table and ate the stew. To me, this was heaven. It was the first time that I had sat with grown-up people. Oh how I wished Eva would let me call Uncle Jack "Daddy", I so wanted a daddy.

We spent all day at the house with Auntie Ethel waiting until her children came home from school. My cousins Irene and Elsie came first. They were both older than me, seven and nine years of age. Then came George, just fourteen years of age and about to leave school the next term. Finally, Reggie and Ronald, twin boys aged twelve arrived, later than the others because they had been selling evening papers. It was very exciting, they were all talking at once. After tea of bread and jam and a cup of milk, Auntie took Eva and me to her next-door neighbour, Daisy. She was a short stout lady with such a lovely laugh it made us laugh as well. As Auntie's house was so full she asked Daisy if we could stay with her. She said that she would be pleased to have us, but it would cost sixpence each with breakfast. After saying goodnight to Auntie Ethel, Daisy got the kettle from the kitchen stove. She stood me in the kitchen sink and washed me all over. That night Eva and I shared a double bed; it was very comfortable and we cuddled up close to one another. I had never felt so happy.

The next morning we waited by the front door to say goodbye to our cousins as they went off to school. Auntie gave Mother some egg sandwiches and told her and Uncle Jack that she hoped that they would find something suitable soon. She also said they should get Eva and me off to school quickly otherwise they would have the School Board man after them. We all said goodbye and again set off to look for a place to live. We walked up Holloway Road towards Highgate and called at several lodgings in the Junction Road area. Still not having any luck, we made our way up Highgate Hill. It was a steep hill and my legs were aching. On the way up, there was a horse trough on the side of the road and I watched some horses stop and have a drink. I asked Eva if I could have some water but she said that we were going to the park to eat our sandwiches and she would get me a drink there. Waterloo Park was lovely with lots of hilly green fields that were great fun to roll down, which Eva let me do. At the bottom of the hill there was a pond with lots of ducks and swans. We had our sandwiches and shared two apples between the four of us and Eva lifted me up to the water fountain for the promised drink. We went on our way again, still looking for a place to sleep that night.

After several more unsuccessful calls Uncle Jack said to Mother that nowhere would take us because of Eva and me, and this started an argument. Mother got very cross. I don't know how long they argued, but we eventually continued our journey. We walked up Highgate Hill and at the top we could see the City. Eva pointed out St Paul's Cathedral to me and I could see the big round dome. That day we must have walked for ages and I don't know how many houses we visited. By evening time I was very tired and walked along with my eyes closed until Eva picked me up and passed me to Uncle Jack, asking him to carry me.

The next morning I found myself in a very long bed. I was wearing a large white nightdress. I saw lots of women putting on the dark blue dresses that I had seen before, with high collars and long sleeves and the flat white caps. My bed was very high, but I managed to get down and tried to climb on Eva's bed.

'Is this a dormitory?' I asked.

Eva drew me into bed with her.

'Yes, I'm afraid that it is. It's a place where people come when they can't find a place to sleep."

'Will we have to stay here?'

'No, we won't. I'm afraid that we will have to go back to St Mary's.'

'I wish we could go to Auntie Ethel's,' I cried. 'I want to see our cousin that's in a box.'

Eva smiled through her tears.

'Oh, don't worry about that, the baby stays there until it is ready to be born, like the bird's eggs do in their nests.'

For a long time after that, I thought that babies came from an egg that was kept warm in a box. Mother appeared, carrying our breakfast on a tray. She was also wearing the workhouse uniform. I stayed with Eva on her bed to eat the porridge and drink the mug of tea. Mother told Eva that she was sorry that this had happened and Eva said crossly,

'You should have looked for lodgings before fetching us. What am I going to tell my friends at school? I told them that I was going home.'

Mother explained that as soon as the Governor of our home had heard that she and Uncle Jack were courting, he had turned us out saying that they were unable to keep us girls if they were to get married. They were not given a chance to say that they didn't intend to get married straight away and it had all happened too quickly. Eva was not at all pleased and said,

'This wouldn't have happened if Uncle Jack hadn't visited you in the women's quarters, both of you broke the rules.'

While Mother and Eva were talking, I looked out of the window and could see men working in the garden and the green van that carried people to different places of work. Some of the men I recognised from St Mary's and the others from the local infirmary. Then I noticed Uncle Jack. He was also wearing the workhouse uniform, a badly fitted grey flannel suit, the same as the other men. He was stacking some large loaves of bread in the van. I banged on the window to wave to him, but he did not hear me. I ran to Eva to tell her, but she was crying and Mother told me to leave her alone.

Later that day we were driven back to St Mary's in the green van, accompanied by a Workhouse Officer and the loaves of bread Uncle Jack had loaded. I was not looking forward to the journey but as I was sitting on Eva's lap it was more comfortable. We were taken straight to the Sick Bay as before but this time Eva weighed and bathed me and tucked me under the bedclothes to wait for the school garments to be fitted. The next morning, we were examined by Dr Jenkins and I said that I did not want to be vaccinated again. Doctor told Nurse Ayres that we were both fit for school and could be discharged straight away. He waited for us to get dressed and walked Eva and me back to Maxwell House. We were just in time to get in line for dinner. Eva returned to the senior girls and our lives went on as though we had never been away.

With one exception, Mother and Uncle Jack never came to visit Eva and me again. They could have come once every two months, when the Workhouse van came, but I think that they may have been refused access to us.

PART TWO

All Change

On the last day in the infants' class at school our teacher, Miss Brown, gave us a party. We played games all afternoon and had sweets to eat. It was while Miss Brown was wishing us a happy summer holiday that Eva came in and asked for permission to take me upstairs. There were ever so many stairs to climb and on the way up Eva told me that she taking me to see her favourite teacher, Miss Parker. We stopped for a few minutes because the big girls were coming out of the classrooms and this gave us time to talk. Eva said that now she was fourteen years old she had to leave school. She would not be seeing me in the playground anymore and she would no longer be working in Maxwell House. I was very worried and asked if I would be seeing her again.

'Oh yes' she said 'but not so often.'

I was now a big girl of seven years old, I was to be good, not get into trouble and I would enjoy all the new things I had to do.

Miss Parker was a very tall and prim lady. Her grey hair was worn in a plait around her head. She had blue twinkling eyes and was wearing a pretty green dress with a lace collar and cuffs. She was cleaning the blackboard when we arrived. She smiled and said

'So this is your little sister. Oh, but how small! Are you sure she is seven years old?' Eva said ,

'Oh yes, she had a birthday two weeks ago and they said that she was seven. They tell me that she is so small because she will not eat her dinners, but then everybody says that most of us at St Mary's are too thin.' Miss Parker looked at me rather sternly and said that this would not do at all; I would have to eat my dinners if I was coming to the big school so I could work hard at my lessons. I nodded that I understood. Miss Parker sat down and drew me closer to her. She said

'We do not nod when we are spoken to. You should say, "*yes Miss Parker*". She then asked about myself. I told her that I could write my name and do sums, that I could do the *Charleston* and that Eva gave me rides on her shoulders just like a flying angel. Miss Parker said

'No wonder she isn't eating, she hasn't any teeth.'

Eva explained that I had had some pulled out a week or two before. I told Miss Parker about going to the Receiving Room and being strapped in a big chair while my hands were being held and the dentist pulled out my teeth. I told her that I had cried a lot. I don't think this kindly lady wanted to hear the gory details and she said

'After you have had your holiday and come back to school, I'm sure that you will have some nice new teeth.'
She wished us goodbye, kissed Eva and told her to come and visit whenever she could.

There was no ceremony or excitement in being transferred to the 'big girls' department at St. Mary's. Officer Welsh came to fetch us from Maxwell House and we went to see Nurse Ayres, the Senior Officer who saw all the new admissions. She was a delightful elderly lady wearing the usual uniform of the other Officers, but had a white starched bow under her chin, and a beautiful eight-pointed brooch on the corner of her apron. She lived and worked in the Sick Bay so we did not see her very often.

Officer Welsh told her our names and she wrote them down in a book. We were undressed and weighed and given our peg numbers for our towels and flannels in the washing room. My number was fifty and that was the number for all the pegs I used. Officer Welsh also showed us where to stand when we were in line. We settled into our new abode very quickly and for a short while we had a wonderful sense of freedom. For the first time we could go into the playground and to the lavatory on our own.

On our first morning a senior girl called Doris Bailey gave us all cleaning rags and metal polish. Ada and Maud were sent to clean the basin, bath taps and chains as well as the brass knobs and finger plates on the doors. Minnie Ha Ha and I were sent back to Maxwell House and told to clean everything that was brass. There were brass taps in the washroom ;door knobs and finger plates; the brass coal scuttle; the handles of the poker and tongs, and a huge fireguard. At first we liked it, taking great pleasure in how bright we could get things and seeing our faces in the finger plates. But our enjoyment did not last for long and the first breakfast bell always rang before we had finished.

After breakfast, we were sent to the scullery to dry plates. There were two very large sinks where Domestic Officers washed the plates and senior girls collected them from the draining racks and brought them to the benches for us to dry. The benches were very high and they had to find some stools for us to stand on. We took plates into the dining hall, placed them into the hot plates and then went back for more. The plates were quite heavy- they were thick white earthen ware- and I could only carry five at a time. If we broke any we had to clear up the pieces and take them to the Domestic Officer who would slap the front of your arm. The number of slaps coincided with the number of broken plates. We would work in the scullery until the school bell was rung.

There were about twenty seven to eight year olds working in the scullery after each meal, most of us drying plates, mugs and cutlery. The boys were busy scrubbing out the huge boilers that were used to cook porridge and vegetables. They rubbed the steel lids with emery paper, and polished the brass taps and the surrounding brass bands. They also cleaned and polished the hot plates. The dining-hall and kitchen area was a beehive of child labour after each meal. It was very difficult to get tidied for school, in fact, this seldom got done. After working in the scullery in the evening, we had to go and clean our boots and report any buttons missing from our pinafores and dresses but again this seldom got done because often we were too afraid to report any tears in our clothes.

Minnie was always in trouble for getting her pinafore and dress dirty: somehow she put more metal polish on herself than on the taps! Also, she would get ink on her fingers and spill paint on her pinny. The poor girl got into trouble many times, but I was nearly as bad: my hands were always black with metal polish. Somehow I did not make such a mess of my blue serge dress as she did. One day after breakfast, Minnie did not come into the scullery with us and no one knew what had happened to her. We had not seen her disappear when we were in the school line. Maud told Officer Hopkins that Minnie was missing. She replied that Minnie had been sent to Matron's office because the assistant Matron, Miss Parsley, had got tired of her dirty clothes. As we were marching up the drive to school, there was Minnie waiting outside the sewing rooms with Miss Parsley. Minnie looked awful; she had obviously been crying a lot and her eyes looked very red and swollen. Poor Minnie was wearing a piece of sacking kept together with black tape tied around her waist. She was pushed towards us to get into line. We were all absolutely shocked and stunned. When we had passed into the street we walked each side of minnie so that the outside people did not see her. We were so ashamed of what they had done to her. When we got to school, Maud told our teacher, Miss Brown, that Minnie was not well and did not want to come into the classroom. Miss Brown could see that something was wrong and asked if Minnie had had an accident and torn her dress.

'We don't know" said Maud

'She was sent to school like that'.

Miss Brown told us that she trusted us not to make any noise and to go into assembly quietly and she took Minnie to see Miss Pugh, the headmistress. Later, when we got home for dinner Minnie was wearing a clean dress. She told us that she had sat by the fire in Miss Pugh's office and a prefect had brought her a cup of warm milk, then taken her home with a note from Miss Pugh.

That evening after tea, before vespers were said, we had a lecture from the Master, Mr Jacobs. From his long lecture we gathered that he was fully responsible for us and that he was answerable to no one; as an acting parent he had every right to punish us as he and his staff thought fit. When we were having a bath that night, Minnie cried when she got into the water. It made her back sting and feel sore. Doris was shocked when she saw Minnie's back. It was black and blue. Eva came into the Bathroom, took Minnie out of the bath and dried her, and said that she would take her straight to bed. When we arrived in the dormitory Eva was sitting with Minnie asleep on her lap. Eva had her head bent downwards and I could see that she was crying. After we had undressed and said the Lord's Prayer, Eva tucked Minnie into bed and kissed her goodnight. She then came over to me, sat on my bed and held me close to her,

"Oh Darling" she said,

'Do promise me that you will be a good girl'.

I held Eva very tightly and also cried. I could feel her fear for me. I promised that I would be good and not get into trouble. She told me that very soon she would be leaving St Mary's to go into service, and she did not know what was to become of me, I was such a little 'pickle'. As she was tucking me into bed, Doris Bailey called,

'Come on Eva, its time the lights were out".

One or two of the girls called goodnight to Eva. She stopped and tucked them in, saying,

'Hush go to sleep.'

'No more talking', said Doris Bailey and they were gone.

The next morning, when Minnie and I went to clean the brass, Eva was there. She had found some old pinafores and made us wear them and she had also got hold of some cleaning rags. She told us that we need not put metal polish on the knobs every day as often a good rub was all that was needed. This helped a lot and we finished earlier.

I don't think that Minnie never got over this episode. She no longer laughed, she was morose, and for a while, unsociable. She would rock herself to sleep at night and grind her teeth. She seemed afraid of us as well as of the Officers. Poor Minnie. What had they done to her? She was no longer called Minnie Ha Ha, but Minnie Mouse.

Eva Goes Into Service

Eva was the tallest girl in the school. She was very graceful and good looking. She was fourteen years of age, had left school, and stopped working at Maxwell House and was to be trained for domestic service. I now saw very little of her. Service, Eva had explained to me, was working for your living by serving other people. She said that if you were good at your work, and liked by the matron, you could be sent to a nice household where the Master and Mistress were good to their employees. She said that when you are older, if you misbehave yourself, they will not only give you a good hiding, but a lot of scrubbing and hearth stoning to do on a Saturday or Sunday afternoon. Later on I did see this happen, but not to me or my friends, thank goodness.

Eva was chosen to work in Mr and Mrs Jacobs the Matron and Master's house This was considered a plum job, as only capable, good girls worked there. She was told to wear her plaited hair around her ears. They looked like earphones and made her look much older. It also meant I could not pull her plaits anymore when I wanted to attract her attention! She had to wear a uniform that looked very much like the Officer's: in the morning, a blue cotton frock with white cuffs and collar, and a large white apron, although she did not have to wear a white cape. In the afternoon Eva looked lovely in a brown frock with coffee-coloured lace collar and cuffs with a little cap to match. Mrs Jacobs employed a full-time maid in her house called Clare; she and Eva became great friends. Eva was told that she would be helping Clare, but it was Clare who had a much easier life than Eva. She had two hours off duty every afternoon, one half day a week, and was finished from 4pm on Sundays. She was also paid wages.

Eva's duties were very much full-time all the time. Each morning she cleaned and lit the dining room fire and the kitchen boiler. Then she hearthstoned the front doorstep. After breakfast, she cleaned and swept the red carpets on the stairs and polished the brass rods and banisters. She then scrubbed the front hall and passages, and polished the hall furniture. She was very often late for dinner, but nobody took any notice. After having her meal, Eva would return to work She had dinner things to wash up and the kitchen table and floor to scrub. She would then change into her afternoon uniform and return to the house to make and serve tea. She was never allowed to wait at the table. Sometimes she had some supper herself, this was a great privilege. She often did not finish work before eight o'clock and as I went to bed at 7 pm, I very seldom saw her; just now and again in the dining hall. One night Eva came to see me when I was still awake and I noticed how tired she looked. And when she cuddled me her hands felt very rough. I looked at them, they were very red and chapped with little cuts on the tips of her thumbs. She saw me looking at them and said that Clare had given her some melrose to put on her hands. I never heard her grumble, somehow Eva managed to take it all in her stride.

Meanwhile, my friends and I settled down to our lessons at school and our routine work in the house without much trouble. However, one day in the dining hall, I could see Thomas on the opposite side and he was opening and closing one eye at me. So I copied. At first, I found it difficult, so I put my hand over one eye and opened and shut the other eye and laughed. Suddenly I got a big smack on the side of my head from the back; I yelled. Officer Welsh, in a loud voice so that everyone could hear, complained that I was winking at the boys. Matron, Eva and the other Officers came to the scene. Matron was very cross and she told Eva that I would be in great trouble if I was not corrected now. I was to be severely punished. I was stood underneath the bell rope in disgrace and went without my meal. Later that evening, when I had undressed ready for bed, Officer Welsh took great delight in giving me what she called "a good smacked bottom". The next time I went into the dining-hall I had to sit with my back to the boys. A box on the ears, or a smacked bottom happened frequently, but we soon got over it.

My first year in the big girls' school soon passed and along came the summer holiday with our two weeks at Dover Court Bay. One of the great highlights was travelling by train, but we used to have to march behind our band to the station. We must have looked a sight as there were at least three hundred of us children. All the local people and our friends at school used to follow us all the way to Highbury to cheer us off. We hated this part of the journey though. When we got to Dover Court Bay we always felt so free. We had no work to do, we could leave our boots and woollen stockings off and run about in bare feet. As far as I can remember we always had lovely summer weather.

One day during the holiday while we were playing on the beach, Eva got a message to go and see Matron at the hotel where she was staying. We wondered if Eva had done something wrong. However, Eva was delighted to see her old school mistress, Miss Parker. She had come from London to ask Eva if she would like to work for her as a live-in maid. Eva was pleased to accept and Matron agreed to the arrangement. Later Miss Parker, Matron and Eva came to the beach where I was playing. Miss Parker called to me. She had a camera that looked like a little black box. I sat with Eva on the cliff and we had our photo taken. This was the only picture that I had taken of me as a child and I still have it today. Miss Parker then told me that she was taking Eva away to London the very next day because she was going to live with her. I was stunned. I just could not believe that this teacher, whom I liked so much, would take Eva away from me. Eva had often told me that she would have to go away one day into service, but somehow I had not taken it in. I asked Miss Parker if I could come and live with her as well. She replied that I still had to go to school, but she was sure that I could visit one day and have a cup of tea with them. Matron told me not to be a silly child and she told Eva to go with Miss Parker to the station the next day. Miss Parker said that as I was now eight years old, I was a big girl and I would be so busy with my lessons at school that I would not miss Eva. She shook hands with us both, told Eva to be ready at 10 o'clock the next morning, then said goodbye. Eva turned to me and said,

'Let us walk along the sea front, it is still quite early'.

I felt very unhappy. This had certainly upset a lovely holiday. The weather was in sympathy with my feelings, it had grown very dark and cold and the wind was blowing the dry sand against my legs, and it stung. The sea looked very angry and I could see a boat tossing about.

We felt little drops of rain and Eva picked me up, sat me on her shoulders with her hands coming up to meet mine. This was the last 'flying angel' I can remember Then we headed back to the camp. As we went on our way Eva told me that Miss Rose had three sisters. They were Miss Margaret, a post office mistress; Miss Eileen, a school teacher, and Miss Jessie, who stayed at home to do the cooking. Eva would have four ladies to look after.

Later, back at the camp we slept in a large hut with our mattresses very close together on the floor which we loved. That night I told Minnie, and anybody else listening, all about Eva and Miss Parker. I embroidered it a bit, saying that Eva was going to a beautiful house with a lovely garden, and that one day I would go and stay with her and would be bought lovely clothes, lots of toys and other things.

During the night it was very windy, the windows rattled and doors banged. There was thunder and lightening and I was unable to sleep. Eva came in and saw that I was awake. She took me to her bed and I slept cuddled up to her till morning. When we woke she said that she would not be coming to say goodbye as she did not want any tears. Instead I was to go with the others to the beach to play and not try to see her. We had a long hug and a kiss and then I did as I was bid. During my play on the beach I did forget about Eva, but when I went to bed that night I could not help but think about her. I wondered whether she would have to work ever so hard. I had heard so many stories about how badly some girls were treated in service. In fact, some had run away from their employers and one or two had returned to St Mary's despite knowing she would be blamed for what had happened. Later that night I woke up crying and a big girl, called Majorie, was cuddling me. She told me that she had been in Miss Rose's class at school and that she was a very kind lady. She said she felt sure that Eva would be very happy and in fact everybody thought what a lucky girl she was. After a while I went off to sleep and just longed for the day when Eva would visit me.

Our Daily Bread

I was eight years of age when I was sent with seven other girls to work in the dining hall. We had to start at 6am, having been woken by the first bell at 5.45. We hardly had time to wash and make our beds before we started in the bread room spreading bread with margarine ready for that day's tea. We had prepared the breakfast bread the evening before. At 6.45 one of us would stay behind to clear up the crumbs and wash the table and floor while the others went into the dining-hall to serve breakfast. We put half a round of bread on each plate, served the porridge into soup dishes, then placed them on the table. The Officers made the urns of tea and put them on the trolley which we wheeled to the end of each table. The next bell was rung at 7am followed by the breakfast bell at 7.10am when the children would march into breakfast. After breakfast, we swept down the tables and the floor, washed and dried the spoons and laid the tables for dinner. We really had to hurry as we had to be out of the dining-hall by 8.10 am to get ready for school and be in line for 8.20. We did much the same after all meals and our routine work was not finished until we had prepared the bread for the next morning's breakfast.

I enjoyed working in the dining hall. The Domestic Officers, Chaff and Cousins, were very kind, easy going and friendly. I think that they worked as hard as we did. They used to cut the bread loaves on a slicing machine, carry the trays into the dining-hall, and help us if we were behind with our work.

When laying the tables, we always knew what cutlery to put out because our diet from week to week was never altered. Every morning it was porridge with half a slice of bread and a mug of tea. At tea, a whole round of bread with a mug of tea. (Sometimes, on a Sunday we would have currant bread, but this was not spread with margarine.) Our dinner menu was as follows:-

Monday - meat, greens, potatoes and rice pudding.

Tuesday - stew, no pudding.

Wednesday - suet pudding with treacle, no first course.

Thursday - stew, no pudding.

Friday - meat, greens, potatoes and rice pudding.

Saturday - stew.

Sunday - cold meat and potatoes, prunes and custard.

Not really a bad menu, except that it was cooked so badly. The meat was cut into very thick lumps and we really felt ill when we saw the blood pouring out. The potatoes were never peeled, the boys used to open the sacks onto the scullery floor with the water tap running, then they did their best to get the soil off with a yard broom. The potatoes were then shovelled into net bags and placed into a big boiler. It was the same with the cabbages; they were never cut open, but were put whole into net bags and boiled. Sometimes the potatoes were horrible, they smelt awful and were black and rotten and the cabbages were full of caterpillars. I only enjoyed Wednesdays and stew days.

At this time I was getting on well at school. Maud and I went into the A class of the third form which was called the scholarship class. Our teacher was Mrs Gloucester MA. She said that she was glad to have girls from the children's home and hoped that we would work hard. At first, Maud and I liked it very much, that is until we were given homework to do. Mrs Gloucester was very cross with us because we never got it done. We had to stay in at playtime and work. Then she reported us to Mrs Pugh, the Headmistress. She even came home with us one evening to speak to Matron. Matron was very annoyed about this and told Maud that we could not be treated differently from the other children and that the school should not interfere with our upbringing. Mrs Gloucester was then very understanding and sympathetic. She explained that if she helped us to get a scholarship and perhaps a place at the secondary school Matron would have to agree that we stayed on at school until we were sixteen. However, we had to leave the home at fifteen years of age, with a year's domestic training so it was not possible. Even so she said that she liked having us in her class and the Headmistress said that we could stay. We spent a lovely year helping all we could, we gave out the papers and filled the inkpots and were so pleased that we did not have homework to do. But of course, we did not realise what we were missing.

At home there was always something to do in the evenings. Three times a week, after we finished our routine work, we had to go into the sewing room to darn stockings or to stitch on buttons. Once a week we had physical training. We used to learn marching formations and do exercises with clubs and dumb bells. Once a month I would have to go and get my hair cut. Everybody's hair was the same style, except one or two who had permission to wear it long. Our hair was cut very short and trimmed at the neck with clippers and kept off the face with a hairband made of black tape and elastic. On the last Monday in the month we went to the *Band of Hope* classes. We used to enjoy singing boisterous songs like *Temperance Boys and Girls We Are* and *Yield not to Temptation*. We were told sad stories about bad men and women who neglected their homes and children because they drank beer. By the age of nine I had signed the Pledge. I did not fully understand, but I wanted the certificate and the picture book that went with it. The certificate was very pretty with a picture of a lovely house in a garden of flowers, with the words 'I promise to abstain from all intoxicating drinks and will help others to do the same'.

Sometimes Eva used to come and see me when I came out of school, but she could only stay for a few minutes as I would get into trouble if I was late. One Sunday after Sunday School she got permission, with Miss Parker's help, to take me to her place of work for tea. She showed me her bedroom with her own wardrobe and chest of drawers. She said that although she was kept busy, it was easier than working in the Matron's house. Miss Parker came into the kitchen while we were having tea. I was enjoying toasted bread with butter and jam. It was heavenly, I had never tasted such lovely food. After tea, Miss Parker showed me the garden where there was a pond with waterlilies and goldfish. She told me the name of the flowers and held me up to feel the sticky buds on the trees. But it all ended too soon as Eva had to walk me back by 7pm. On the way she told me that Miss Parker was doing her best to find Mother some work where she could 'live in' and then she could leave the workhouse. This was great news as I hated thinking of Mother in those awful clothes although I had not seen her for such a long time. I did not know then that I would be seeing mother soon and what a catastrophe it was going to be.

Mother did leave the workhouse and she got a job as an undercook in a large house in Hampstead. Although I was pleased for her, I was also disappointed because Eva gradually stopped coming to see me instead she used to spend her half days with Mother. She wanted to keep an eye on her and help her. For a while, I felt heartbroken, I so longed for Eva to come and visit me, but she said that Mother took up all of her time.

The Inspection

We children made our own fun and games whenever we could. We used to have races while laying the tables, or see who could lay the straightest line of mugs. Miss Chaff and Miss Cousins did not mind this as long as the work got done. We also made up poetry and songs. One song we were fond of singing was:

At six o' clock every morn
we start our busy day.
We stoke the stoves, and greased the loaves
and cleared the crumbs away.
We washed the jugs, and wiped the mugs
and filled the urns with squash,
and tenderly dripped the porridge flop
into everybody's dish.
Oh! orderly orderly orderly day,
ring the bell for school so we can run away.

One morning while we were singing and making more noise than usual, we were surprised at the entrance of the Master and Matron with lots of other people. We stopped what we were doing immediately and stood to attention. Mr Jacobs spoke to us more kindly than usual and told us to,

'Carry on the good work.'

The visitors came round and spoke to every one of us. They asked questions like 'How old are you?' 'Have you been here long?' 'What are you having for breakfast today?', and so on. Then they left us and went round the rest of the building. At breakfast there was much excitement with all of us telling each other what we had been asked. For once the officers did not stop us from talking.

Usually the children that wet their beds stood with their faces to the wall by the bell rope, holding their wet sheets and going without breakfast. But on this occasion, they were told to take their sheets to the laundry before breakfast, and were allowed to sit down for the meal. The visitors were still in the building when we came home for dinner, and again in the evening and they stayed until we had all gone to bed. The Officers must have known that we were going to have visitors because they looked smarter than usual and they were on duty before breakfast. As a rule we did not see them until they checked us out for school. That morning I saw Officer Welsh actually bend down and tie up a little girl's shoelaces. Any other time she would have boxed her ears. We were unable to find out who these visitors were, nobody seemed to know, not even the Officers would tell us. We could see that they were very annoyed at this intrusion and they seemed to think that it was the teachers' fault. Forever after this was known as the Great Inspection Day.

At school that day, before assembly, Maud told Mrs Gloucester all about our strange visitors and she asked her if she knew who these people were. Mrs Gloucester said that she was as mystified as we were. At four o'clock there was a message to say that all girls were to go to the Headmistress's office to be told about new changes. Miss Parker gave us a talk about a new Committee who had taken over from the Board of Guardians to look after and care for the people of Islington. She told us that we had nothing to worry about and that, in fact, she thought, in time, it would be better for use. However, as far as we were concerned, worked went on as usual. Our routine and our lives did not change. We were kept busy even on Saturdays. In the morning we scrubbed the tables, the brooms and dustpans, we washed the trolleys and oiled the casters. The boys washed out the hot plate ovens and cleaned the tops with emery paper and made them very shiny. They also black-leaded the fire grates and polished the fire guards and fetched the scuttles of coal.

One Saturday each month we stood in line for the cobbler to come and examine our boots. He would walk in front of us and look at the front of our shoes, then round the back picking up our feet as though they were horses' hooves, to see if we needed new tips.

Once a month we were examined by Doctor Jenkins. We had to strip down to our knickers in the wash-house, then go into the play-room and stand and wait while he examined each one of us. The big girls used to feel very embarrassed and turn their backs on us. An

Officer would stand with a tray with a jar of pink stuff on it with a metal tongue depressor. Doctor used this for each of us, it left a funny feeling in the mouth. We were not allowed to talk and although the doors and windows were shut it was often freezing. We could get dressed after we had been examined, and it was often teatime before the last ones got dressed.

If there was no inspection of any kind on a Saturday, we would be taken out for a walk. There would be over a hundred of us with only two Officers. In crocodile file we walked to Finsbury Park and back. This was terribly dull as we could only walk as fast as the little girls. The senior girls were dotted along the line to help push us on our way.

Sundays were spent mainly with religion. When we finished our routine work, we sat down in the day room in silence and read our Bibles. We then got ready for the church service in the Dining Hall at 10.30am. The Vicar, the Rev. Stanley Capps, took the service. Sometimes Mr Jacobs read the lesson. The whole time I was at St Mary's the Vicar seldom spoke to any of us personally and never knew our names. His sermons were very 'highbrow' and we never really understood what he was talking about. Our church was St Mary's in Highbury and once a year we marched along Hornsey Road, behind our Band, to attend service there. How we hated this. As soon as the outside people heard our Band, they would come out and line the streets. Our school pals would shout to us and walk all the way with us, shouting and trying to make us speak to them. We felt that we were on show. I never understood why we had to do this. It was dreadful.

We had outside people from the local Baptist church to take us to Sunday School in the afternoon. They were a lovely group of people. The leader, Mr Richard Kerr, was a scoutmaster. He did not like having Sunday School in the Dining Hall very much, so whenever weather permitted, he would take us into the playground. He and the other teachers would tell us stories about scouting and teach us scout songs. This was the only time the boys and girls mingled with each other. To us it was great fun and something different. If it were not for our Sunday School teachers we would not have known about Harvest Festival. Every year they decorated our Dining Hall with fruit and vegetables and they also gave flowers at Easter and holly at Christmas. Mr Kerr would bring his scout troop at Christmas to entertain us. We joined in the games and tricks that they got up to. Miss Parker was also a Sunday School teacher and took the senior girls for Bible class. She had an orchard at home and would give each child an apple on their way out from Sunday school.

Sunday evening vespers were usually taken by Mr Jacobs after we had our tea. His talks were mostly about our misdemeanours. He was very fond of saying,

'If a man does not work neither shall he eat.'

And he went on to explain that we were taught to use our hands because it would be by labouring that we would have to earn our living when we left. He told us that we would always be poor and that when we left school, life would not be easy. His talk often ended with,

'Keep your hands from picking and stealing and your tongues from evil speaking, lying and slandering.'

At bedtime we were still expected to kneel and say prayers before we got into bed.

It was visiting day for the girls who had left St Mary's on the first Sunday in every month. Eva visited regularly at first, then less and less. On one of these visits she told me that she no longer worked for the Misses Parker because one of the sisters had died and that teachers had had their salaries cut by a whole pound a week. She still remained friends with them and sometimes went there for tea. She was now working as a general maid in a large house in Finsbury Park for a big family. She said that she had to work very hard as there was no other helper. Both the Master and Mistress were out all day as they had a tailor's shop in the East End of London. They had three boys and Eva had to look after them, see them off to school, do the housework and laundry. She did not do the cooking, but she did all the washing up. She told me that the Mistress did not like her and gave her very little time off. However she was usually free on Fridays from 3pm, but even then she had to ask for this time off to come and visit me.

Mother Lets Me Down

One morning I had a postcard handed to me. I had never had any post before. It was a card from Eva. It was not in an envelope, just a picture postcard type. On the front it read *'To Wish you a Happy Birthday'*. I took it to school to show my teacher. She asked me the date of my birthday and she was surprised when I said nobody had ever told me when my birthday was and that this was the first card I had ever had. She smiled and looked in her register and told me that my birthday was on 4th July and that I was born in 1917. That afternoon, when lessons had finished, Miss Gloucester gave me a two penny bar of Cadbury's chocolate. I shared this with Maud as we walked home.

That year, Maud and I went up to the 'A' stream of the fourth form. We met up with Ada and Minnie and some of our other friends. The work was not so interesting, as a lot of it, such as fractions and decimals, we had been doing in the other class. Our teacher, Miss Bosher, was a homely and buxom lady. She was very fond of needlework, which we did a lot, along with knitting and crochet, we also did a lot of art work.

During this period, my work at the home was changed. I moved from the dining hall to work in the dormitories. This work was mainly making the beds, turning all the sheets down to exactly the same length, sweeping and polishing the floors, sorting, counting and listing the clothes and linen that we took to the laundry. On Saturdays we put out clean clothes and on Fridays clean sheets and pillowcases. After dinner, we went to pick up clean linen from the laundry and took it to the sewing room. Here we examined it for mending then refolded it and put it away in the cupboards upstairs. On Saturdays we polished the floors in all four of the girls dormitories. We used the turpentine first as this was to clean the floors. This stuff used to make our hands sting. Then we polished with ronak. We used a big polisher which was a heavy block with a long handle and we would swing this up and down with a duster underneath it. This was quite heavy going. We also cleaned the brass on the doors and in the fireplaces. The fires were never lit, but we kept the grates clean. We also attended to the lavatory on each landing. We cut up newspapers into squares and tied it into bundles for use as toilet paper.

One day, on my way to school in the afternoon, we passed a lot of children looking inside the public house called the Nags Head. There was lots of noise and music and people were jigging about and singing 'Knees up Mother Brown'. I was very curious and stood and watched. Then I got a shock. I could see a large rimmed black hat with bright red cherries on it bobbing up and down, below the hat was a long green coat with torn pockets. It looked very grubby. I wanted to run away, but somehow I was glued to the spot. I had to see if it was her Surely she would be at her place of work at this time? Then she turned and saw me. Her face was all red and her hair untidy. She came outside and spoke to me

'Ow are yer? I've been to see your Matron this morning'.

Her voice was different. She sounded far off and the words were drawled. I did not wait to hear any more, I ran as fast as I could and did not stop until I got to school. I was so shocked, I did not know what to think. I felt so ashamed. How could she go and see Matron looking like that and *why* did she have to go? Fancy drinking beer in a pub. It was not long since I had signed the Pledge. Was it any wonder that I thought my mother a very bad lady? I wondered if any of my friends had seen what happened. I stayed away from them at playtime and hid in the lavatory.

When I came out of school, Eva was standing in the playground. I had forgotten it was Friday. She came over to me quickly and asked if I had seen Mother because they were going to Auntie Ethel's. I burst into tears and I could not speak because I was sobbing. Eva had never seen me like this. She took me back into school and sat with me in the cloakroom. I managed to tell her that I had seen Mother in the pub and she looked awful. Eva did not understand why I was so upset about it. She said that lots of people drink beer now and again. But I couldn't explain what Mother looked like. Then I asked why did she have to see Matron? Eva was stunned. She was quiet for a few minutes then she took me on her lap.

'No dear, I will not let her do this to you.'

'What do you mean' I said. I got down from her lap, shouted and stamped my foot.

'Tell me, tell me'. I sobbed and sobbed. I could not help it. Eva dried my face.

"Come on, I cannot take you out like this" she said. "Please don't worry, I will come home with you and see Matron. I promise that you will not be sent away".

When we got back home, the gates were shut. Eva rang the bell and Mr Ridgeway let us in.

'Hallo!" he said "I was just about to report that you were missing.'

Eva told him that it was her fault and asked for permission to see Matron. She came with me to make our excuses to the Officer in charge, then she left me and went to Matron's office. I did not hear anything about being sent away so I thought everything was all right and I forgot all about it.

The Wonderful London County Council

Shortly after the Great Inspection Day the Committee came to see us again while we were having tea. After Evensong we were told to sit down and to face the front. All the Officers were then asked to come into the dining-hall. We had never seen all the Officers together before especially as the Duty Officer never spoke to the Domestic Officers. As well as the Officers there was Mr Young, who taught music to our Band Boys, the teachers who taught tailoring and cobbling and even the boiler house men and plumbers.

Mr Jacobs then introduced a very plump gentleman with ginger hair and a red face, the Chairman of the London County Council. I cannot remember his name. He got into the pulpit and told us that his Committee was going to take the place of the Board of Guardians. He said the poor and their children would be better cared for in Islington. The speech was very long and I did not understand all that was said, but I do remember a few things. He called our school 'antiquated' and a 'dilapidated decaying building' that should have been closed a long time ago and he also said that his Committee was not going to be 'Guardian of the Purse'. This meant that we would have better clothes and food, and that staff would not be employed for being good disciplinarians alone, but they must also know about the care of children. Also, the detention room was not to be used again for whacking children behind closed doors. When the boys heard this, they went frantic. They clapped their hands and stamped their feet and it was a long time before Mr Jacobs could bring them to order. When it was quiet again, the Chairman began to smile; I think that he knew he was annoying the staff. Then he said,

'I think that we will be able to give you all a penny or two each week.'

One of the boys shouted,

'Three cheers for the London County Council.'

We then all made such a noise with cheering and clapping, that we did not hear the order to stand until the band started to play.

After this, things began to happen very gradually. It started with Mr Jacks, the cobbler. He came one Saturday to measure our feet for sandals. Then, one Sunday morning, Officer Hopkins came round with some rolls of beautiful coloured ribbons. She said that we could wear ribbons on Sunday instead of hairbands and we were even asked what colour we would like to wear. Minnie chose blue. She did look lovely; it went well with her blue eyes and fair hair. I chose yellow because it made me feel so happy. When I saw all the different coloured bows on the girls' heads, I thought they looked so very beautiful that I shall never forget it. Later that evening when Mr Jacobs took the service, he gave us a lecture on wastefulness. He said that we were to fold up the ribbons and place them in our baskets for use next Sunday. He also told us that from the following Saturday we would receive pocket money. All children up to the age of twelve years would have one penny a week, and from twelve onwards, tuppence per week. He emphasised that this was 'merit money' and that meant it had to be earned and anyone misbehaving, not doing their work properly or breaking the rules, would lose their pocket money and get the usual punishment as well.

When we went to Dover Court that year, in 1927, we girls were given printed coloured frocks with knickers to match. I had never really noticed what the boys wore before, but this time they were wearing open-necked pale blue shirts with grey flannel suits. They all looked very smart. The sandals and more comfortable clothes made our holiday at Dover Court extra enjoyable that year and when we returned home, there were further surprises. The decorators had painted our dormitories. Instead of being dark green, the walls were painted yellow and the doors and window frames white. Between each window hung a pretty picture with a gold lettered text on them. Most were pictures of flowers and birds and some had a picture of Jesus with children. I loved those pictures and would walk round and learn all the texts off by heart. Then that evening, although it was still light, Officer Hopkins turned on the lights and they all came on at once, it was magic! Now the lights were hanging from the ceiling. They looked like little heads with Chinese rice hats on them, but they were not so pretty as the gas mantles had been. Those shades had looked like ladies crinoline skirts and when the flames flickered, they looked as if they were dancing. However, we soon got used to the electric light and they were more convenient as it meant we did not have to wait for an Officer to come and light them. All of the buildings went over to electricity, except for the lamps in the drive. I was pleased because I loved to see Mr Reid come along each evening to light the lamps. We would listen for his whistling and when we looked out of the window he would shout goodnight to us.

More changes continued to happen. One that stands out the most was that our boots were changed for black lace-up shoes. I felt very proud of mine and would polish them until I could see my face in them. Green and blue were our school colours and we wore green jumpers with dark blue drill slips and our hairbands were made up with green ribbon. The name of our Home was changed to 'The Andover Children's Home', which was painted in white on the large brown entrance gate. The spikes and pieces of glass, however, were still on top of the wall that surrounded us.

I was sent to the Sick Bay with a message one day and much to my surprise Nurse Saunders answered the door. It was lovely to see her. She gave me a big hug and kissed me. She said that the Council had closed the Receiving Homes and that they were being changed to Clinics for mothers to take their babies to. She, Officer Hassell and two other members of staff, had been transferred to our Home. Nurse Saunders asked me to keep this a secret from my friends as she said that when she came to the dayroom that evening to do routine medicines she wanted to surprise them. I was so excited that I could not keep the secret from Minnie and Ada and together we rounded up the other girls and asked them to come into the dayroom after tea. When Nurse Saunders came in with the medicines they were all so delighted and went running to her, nearly knocking the tray out of her hands. She remembered everybody's names and said that she had often thought about us and hoped that we were being good. She told us that Nurse Ayres was going to retire as she was 72 years old and that she would be taking her place. We were very sorry to hear about Nurse

Ayres although we did not see her very often. She was a very kind person and had worked at St Mary's since 1886. However, we were all so glad that Nurse Saunders was taking her place. Miss Hassell would be looking after the little ones in Maxwell House.

One evening, as I came down the drive from school, I was told to polish my shoes, get washed and go into the sewing room for a clean drill slip. I wondered whatever was happening, I knew that I had not done anything wrong, so was very puzzled. I felt better when I saw some children from Maxwell House being taken to the Matron's office as well. We waited in a little room. I could hear a lot of men's voices while we were waiting. Then Officer Hopkins, looking very smart, asked me to go into the office with her. She took hold of my hand and led me in. There were about four elderly men and Master and Matron sitting round a very highly polished table. Matron told the Officer to sit me on the empty chair at the end. The green leather seated chair was very high and slippery and I had to climb up. My eyes came up to the rim of the table. I sat quietly and looked at the photographs of old men hanging on the walls around the room. Then I noticed that I could see the upside down faces of the people round the table, they looked so funny. There was one gentleman with thick black hair, bushy eyebrows and a black bushy beard. He looked, in the reflection, just like the coconuts I had seen at the fair at Dover Court. When you broke a coconut, milk came out of it, so I was wondering what would happen if this man opened his mouth to speak. One of the other men was bald headed. The light on it made it shine, but the reflection on the table made it look brighter still. It looked like a halo. Miss Hopkins came over and touched my shoulder.

'Pay attention,' she said 'you are being spoken to'.

I looked up and everyone was staring at me.

'Come on,' said Matron sharply, 'answer the question.'

Not knowing what the question was I just said 'I don't know.'

Mr Jacobs said to Matron, 'Is she all there?'

Matron replied that at school they said I was bright. Then the coconut gentleman said to me kindly.

'How old are you dear?'

'I'm ten years old Sir'.

'There you are,' he said, 'she does know her age.'

Then I was told to stand up on the chair as one of the gentlemen could not see me. I found this difficult as the leather sort of moved, so I leant forward with my knees on the edge of the table.

'How old did you say she was? She looks very small. I thought it was only junior children that that we considered for the foster homes.'

Matron then spoke very quickly,

'Yes that is true. However, our number in the house has increased greatly in receiving children from the other homes you have closed. I have sent for some mothers' of the older children to see if they would agree to transfers. This child's mother signed a letter saying that she agreed.'

I started to cry. I then heard Matron say

'Her mother has a bad influence on the child, and now that she has got herself a job, we cannot stop the mother seeing her when she comes out of school. I sent for her and she signed the letter agreeing that we could send her out to be fostered in the country.'

I did not know what to do as I was wriggling because I wanted to go to the lavatory. The coconut gentleman then spoke to me again very kindly.

'Would you not like to go to the country and live in a nice house with foster parents?'

I asked if my friends would come with me and how my sister would know where I was. Then another gentleman asked me if I liked it here and I said,

'Yes Sir and I like school too.'

Then in my nervousness I wet myself and began to cry, saying,

'Please Sir don't let them send me away.'

Matron interrupted the conversation saying to me,

'It is not for you to say where you will go. We have always done the best for you.'

Then the committee all began talking about me, asking Matron if I was well behaved and if she thought that I would settle down in a smaller home. I was suddenly very afraid. I imagined a big green van coming for me and taking me to some terrible place. I knew that these people did not understand about me not wanting any changes. Then Officer Hopkins came over to me and gave me a handkerchief to wipe my eyes. She took hold of my hand to take me away. I pulled my hand away and became hysterical, shouting

'I won't go away. I won't go away.'

Everybody looked shocked, they did not realise that I was actually afraid of most people. I thought that the new people could be as unkind as the Officers in the Home. Officer Hopkins again tried to take me out of the room when one of the gentlemen said,

'Now stop crying there's a good child. Nobody will send you away against your wishes.'

'Thank you Sir' I replied, and with this Officer Hopkins opened the door. That day I did not go into tea, but went straight upstairs to bed and cried myself to sleep.

For the next few days, I was not only miserable but I felt ill as well. My eyes kept watering, people thought I was crying and my mouth was dry and very sore. Miss Bosher sent me home from school with a prefect because I was not well. When I went to the Sick Bay, Nurse Saunders said,

'Come in and join the rest of us, I have twenty five of you in here with measles.'

Me and Eva at Dover Court Bay, 1925

Mother, 1930s

PART THREE

The Closing of the Workhouse Homes

The London County Council started closing a lot of small children's homes and orphanages and were transferring many of the children to St Mary's. More beds were put up in the dormitories and more tables in the dining hall, and our numbers rose from 325 children to 400. This made it very cramped.

Some of the new children were not used to our way of life and they found our hard discipline and rigid routine irksome. Some of them had come from a residential school for backward children, a few of which were quite big children of 13 and 14 years of age. They were very quiet and scared and needed help crossing the road. We had to start out for school earlier because of this or else we would have been late for our classes.

There were other children that were quite the opposite. They were a rough crowd and would use bad language and swear at the Officers. They were cheeky and refused to help with any chores. The Officers were spiteful and hateful towards them and were always warning them of severe punishments. This however, did not appear to affect these new girls and we thought their behaviour was strange. They were bigger and stronger than us which caused a problem when they were punished as they would kick and punch back. I once saw Officer Hopkins sitting on a swearing child on the bathroom floor, while another Officer was forcing carbolic soap into her mouth to wash it out. Another time, two were holding a girl over her bed while Officer Hassell tanned her bare back with a hairbrush. Both Officers had their aprons torn off them, lost their caps and one of them had her glasses broken. When an Officer was confronted with one who would put up a big fight, she would ask any of us to help hold the child if there was no other Officer about. We refused to do this, it was a thing of trust among us, we would never aid in any way. Also, we never told tales about one another. The Officers became more aggressive towards all of us at this time and life for us became almost unbearable.

Mr. Jacobs began to lecture us more often about discipline, with more threats of severe punishments. We were told that although the detention room was closed by order of the new Committee, it would not prevent the cane from being used. We already knew this as we had seen boys being caned in front of the whole school in the dining hall and this was happening more and more often. We found it very upsetting and talked about it among ourselves. The house girls (those over fourteen years old) also disapproved and said that we should put our heads together to try and think of a way of stopping it.

One day after our tea, three boys were standing with their faces to the wall next to the bell rope. Mr. Jacobs gave us one of his lectures, announcing that Mr. Ridgeway was going to punish the boys by giving each one of them six strokes of the cane. He said that the boys had stolen food from the larder the day before and had, that morning, spent the day at Caledonian Market instead of attending school. As well as being caned the boys were to have their shoes taken away from them for the weekend and would lose their pocket money and do extra chores. Mr. Jacobs then left the hall telling Mr. Ridgeway to take over. Mr. Ridgeway made the first boy bend right over a stool so that his hands touched the floor, being very fastidious as to the position of the boy. He then took off his jacket and tested the two canes that had been hanging on the fireguard. He started to cane the boy but when he got to the second stroke, all hell broke out. The senior girls and boys banged their mugs on the table and some boys rushed at Mr. Ridgeway knocking him to the floor, taking the cane from him. The noise was terrific. Officers arrived from the kitchen along with Mr. and Mrs. Jacobs from their house. Mr. Jacobs blew his whistle and shouted for us to stop. He tried to get the boys off Mr. Ridgeway but got knocked down himself. While this was happening, I noticed that the little girls at my table looked very scared and some were crying, so as I was nearest to the exit, I opened the door and let them out, together with some other children. When Mrs. Jacobs saw what I had done, she boxed my ears and sent me back to my place and then pressed the fire alarm. This was a hooter that sounded all over the building.

I had never seen so many Officers come running into the dining hall. Mr. Jacobs had a quiet word with them and then they came and stood at the end of each table. All the infant and junior girls were brought back in while Mr. Jacobs stood in the pulpit looking at us in disbelief. He looked very pale and tense and when he had got over the shock he said that we would all be punished for such bad behaviour and that the boys who had absconded would still receive their flogging along with the boys that started the riot. He blamed the London County Council, saying that he cursed the day that they took over and he got sent the extra wild brats to look after. He called to Mr. Ridgeway to continue his duties in caning the boys, but the boys shouted and began to throw their mugs and plates at the pulpit. Through the shouts we could hear repeated,

'Not in front of the girls', to which many of the Officers agreed and Mr. Jacobs quickly told all the girls to leave the hall.

That evening the three original boys got thrashed, along with many others, but it was the last time that canings were carried out in the dining hall. However, remembering what bullies the boys' Officers were, I am sure that canings continued elsewhere.

There were some boys who were never caned and appeared never to get into trouble, they were our Band Boys. Everyone made a fuss of these lads, not only the Officers, but the girls as well. I can remember saving all the crusts of bread and spreading them with extra margarine to give to the Band Boys when I worked in the dining hall. The boys were kept very busy practising their music and keeping their instruments and uniforms clean, so they never did any other chores. They were popular and very well known outside the school and were hired out for all sorts of festivities: Putney Bridge on Boat Race Day, City of London for the Lord Mayor's Show, and they played at our school on Empire Day. They looked very smart in their green uniforms and we were very proud of all the boys. When there was any special day coming, we could hear them practising until the early hours of the morning. The boys were very fond of the band master, Dr Love. He was a tall, smart, clean shaven man with a thick mop of curly red hair. He was a strict and exacting teacher, but a very fair and kindly man, who stood up for the boys and protected them from any bullying.

In 1931, during my last year at day school, we put on HMS Pinafore for the end of term concert. Dr Love heard about the show and thought it would be a good idea if we could join the boys to give a performance to the LCC Committee at Christmas. Mr. Jacobs was not in favour but Dr Love managed to get round him. The show was performed to the Committee of the LCC and to the children in our dining hall on New Year's day. In the show Maud took the part of Buttercup and Minnie and I danced the sailor's hornpipe in the chorus.

In 1932 there were only fifty boys left at St Mary's and it appeared obvious that it was soon to close down. Dr Love left us and we all felt this loss greatly. The boys cried openly and the whole school seemed sad. The Boy's Band had been the loveliest thing at St Mary's, we had all enjoyed marching to the band and listening to it, especially when we camped at Dover Court Bay. I believe that Dr Love went into the Army where a lot of his boys were eventually sent as cadets.

Extra Work

The year was 1929 and Maud and Ada had their twelfth birthdays in June, with mine in July and Minnie's in August. Now we were twelve, we were old enough to take more responsibilities such as helping to look after the little ones. Maud and I were sent to Maxwell House where there were already four others helping. Minnie went to the dining hall, as the senior girl, and we thought her very lucky. Ada spent most of her time in the sewing room sorting out clothing and darning stockings. It had been found that Ada had a weak heart, so she was not allowed to do any strenuous work.

At Maxwell House, there were three officers; Bishop, Jackson and Brown. Officer Hassell worked as a relief for their days off and was at the girls' department for the rest of the week. I was looking forward to working with the little ones, I got on well with them and enjoyed singing and playing games, when I had time. All of the helpers had started life in Maxwell House at St Mary's, so we were already familiar with the routine. I thought that the Officers were nicer to us helpers than they were to the infants. It seemed that they would never speak to them kindly or offer any encouragement to them.

Officer Hassell was worse, however, as she was not nice to anyone. She was a very disagreeable person, was hard to the infants, bullied us helpers and did not appear to get on with the other officers. Everybody was afraid of her. She used to boast that she was a good disciplinarian and had been sent to St Mary's to 'smarten us up'. She would come and strip the beds and make us redo them, saying that they had not been turned down to the same length, or the bed casters were not in a straight line. Often she would complain that the children's shoes were not bright enough and make one of us clean all fifty-five pairs again. Even when we were about to leave with the children for school, she would call us back and say that the playroom was filthy and we would have to sweep and dust it again. When this happened we would receive black marks at school for being late. The other Officers were too afraid to say anything, but we got used to this silly woman. She slept in a cubicle at the end of the infant's dormitory, so we would annoy her by getting the children up early to disturb her sleep. Also, on her day off, we would make as much noise as possible kicking the bed castors straight. When she kept us working late in the evening, we would try and make it as late as possible by putting out the clean clothes on the foot of the beds. When she spent the rest of the week in the girls' department it was heavenly for us all at Maxwell House.

Minnie, Ada, Maud and I were now in the fifth form at school. On arrival every morning we would be given cod liver oil and malt, along with the other 'outside' girls. We felt guilty about this as it was meant for poor children and we never thought of ourselves as poor. Minnie and Ada were in the 'B' class and Maud and I were in the 'A' class. We saw a lot of each other however as we attended the same cookery, laundry and housewifery classes. Our cookery teacher, Mrs Standish, must have thought us 'home' girls an ignorant lot as we had never heard of or seen many of the vegetables, fruits or the dishes used. Once she took six of us to the shops in Seven Sisters Road and showed us round a large grocer's shop, a greengrocer's and a chandler's. I had never been into shops of these kind before and was still shy when going into a sweet shop to ask for a ha'porth of toffee or stickjaw. There were also many other things that I did not know about. I had never seen a postman or received an unopened letter; had never seen or been inside a Post Office or stuck a stamp on an envelope; I had never been on a bus or tram and had never seen a newspaper. It must have been very difficult for our teachers as we children from St Mary's just did not know about the outside world. When we started to do monetary sums, we had great difficulty as we had never heard anyone talking about pounds, shillings and pence. Nobody had explained to us where food and clothes came from or how much they cost. Our food and clothes were always provided. We had missed out a great deal on everyday experiences and conversations.

At thirteen years old I was still working at Maxwell House as the senior helper. I had been there for the longest period, so more was expected of me and most of my time outside school was spent there. I had become quicker and better at getting my routine jobs done, so I had more time to sing and play with the children.

Once a fortnight the Officers cut the children's hair. We did not have a hairdresser or barber and when the boys had their hair cut it looked as though a basin had been used! Their hair was left in a circle at the top of their head and clipped to the back and sides, so they looked like tiny monks. The girls' hair was always cut straight, no fringes or curls allowed, and the hair brushed off the face with hair bands. On Sunday we were allowed to wear ribbons. I could not tie a ribbon on my hair so I always wore a hair band. Eva once gave me and my friends some pretty hair bands of blue ribbon with little pink rosettes on the sides, that she had made. We had to get permission to wear them and we were only allowed to wear them on Sundays.

As I got older, I saw the true relationship between the Officers and the children. Most of the Officers were unapproachable and appeared stand-offish. They seldom talked to us and when they did it was mostly to find fault with our work or give us further orders. They seemed to think that if a child had plenty of work to do and was provided with just enough food to keep them from starving, clothes and shelter, that was all that was necessary. There were some Officers who treated us with varying degrees of severity, such as beating us for slight misdemeanours and depriving us of any little pleasure. It seemed that they were irritated by us and resented our presence, it was rare to be shown any kindness. They perhaps could not be entirely blamed for this as this sort of cruelty went all the way down the line; Senior Officers bullied the junior staff who in turn bullied the senior girls and boys and the seniors bullied the little ones. It appeared that the staff were employed only if they were good disciplinarians and their understanding of discipline was taken from Mr. Jacobs, the Headmaster.

It used to worry me sick when any of the infants got spanked, especially when they had done nothing wrong, like crying on bath nights. We only had to tell the little ones to undress ready for a bath and they would start crying. When they had their hair washed their heads would be pushed backwards under the water. Green soft soap used to be washed well down onto their faces and into their eyes and then large jugs of cold water were poured over them to rinse their hair. The sudden rush of cold water gave them an awful fright and caused them to gasp for breath. If a child screamed it was given a hard slap for making a fuss. This nightmarish experience affected all of us and we helpers would get up to all sorts of tricks and make excuses not to help on bath nights. To see these little children shake with fear, cringe or run away just because they were going to have a bath was terrible. When you managed to pick them up to undress them, they would cling on to you so tightly it hurt. There was no one to talk to about this as it looked as though we were being silly about children who did not like their baths. This awful cruelty has affected my whole life and to this day I cannot bear to see a child in pain or being hurt in any way.

At school I went up into the top class. There were more students in this class as there were no 'A' or 'B' sections. We had two class teachers, Miss Parker, who was also the Assistant Head, and Miss Bosher. Maud was voted in as Head Girl. This was a great honour as it was the first time a 'Home' girl had been chosen. Minnie and I were two of the six prefects. Each of the prefects was responsible for a particular job; mine was to look after the plants in the main hall and Minnie looked after the hymn books and got the music ready at the piano. As well as this, we made sure that the students obeyed the whistle and got into their class lines after playtime.

In class I shared a desk with an 'outside' girl, Lesley, who was tall, thin and pale with lanky unkempt hair. She was the middle child of five and was very poor. She lived at the back of the school in a small, two-up two-down, house. Her father was a semi-invalid who had been injured in the Great War and was often out of work. Her mother worked early in the mornings scrubbing front door steps. Lesley was often late for school because she had to wait for her mother to come home from work, so she could wear her shoes. I liked Lesley very much, she was bright and jolly. She was unpopular with the others though as she smelt so badly and always had nits. Lesley had been with Maud and me in the scholarship class. She had sat and passed the entrance exams for Central School but her parents could not afford the uniform, so she was unable to go there. At times I envied Lesley; she cared a lot for her younger brother and sister and always spoke lovingly of

65

her Mum and Dad. It must be lovely to have someone to love and to be loved all the time.

As the term went on I began to fall behind in my school work. I came twenty fifth from the top in class and had quite a few black marks for being late. Miss Parker told me that she was disappointed with my last report and asked if Matron had spoken to me about it. I was surprised as I had not realised that I had been so bad. Miss Parker read my report to me; it said that I was withdrawn and pallid; that I stuttered when answering questions and was physically backward for my age. I did not understand what it all meant, except I did understand the word 'backward' and it worried me. Miss Parker asked if there was anything worrying me and after a long chat she said she would ask the Headmistress if I could have some extra lessons, after school, in singing and speech. I told her that I would get into trouble if I stayed late as I had to help take the infants home. She replied,

'You and the others like you are little women, you have never been allowed to be children.'

From that time onwards, Miss Parker endeared herself to me. She took the English literature class, introducing me to the English poets and their work. This was to give me a life long love of poetry. I joined the school choir and was allowed to stay on after school to practise once a week. We children that had speech difficulties at school were given elocution lessons by Miss Ross and were taken to the main hall and individually made to read out loud. Often I was asked to read the lesson for assembly. However, when I got home to Maxwell House, there was still work for me to do there.

News About Mother

When Eva came to see me she asked why I was not doing so well at school. She said that Miss Parker had written to her and asked if it was possible for her to visit me more often. Eva had another job in a much nicer house with only two people to look after. She told me that Wednesday was her half day and that she would meet me at 4.30pm each week, and also that she would visit me on 'old girls Sunday', once every two months. This was lovely news and I felt much happier. I asked her how Mother was as I had not seen her for ages and ages. Eva gave a wry smile and said that she herself did not see Mother much now either. She said that Mother had found some new friends and visited them on her time off. After Eva's visit my school work started to improve and at the end of the next term I had crept up to twelfth place in class.

One day in class Miss Bosher asked us eight 'home' girls if we received any pocket money and if so, what we did with it. We told her that we seldom got our tuppence each week as it was often stopped if we had done something wrong, such as not doing our work properly or being late on line. In fact, I had never received my tuppence, but I did not say so. A few evenings later we were not surprised to receive a lecture from Mr Jacobs about telling tales in school. He informed us that the money was merit money, *not* pocket money and that if it was stopped it was entirely our fault. He said that it was nothing to do with our school teachers and he wanted to know what they were planning to *do* with our merit money. He then told us that our money was put into a Post Office savings account for us to receive when we left the home. Some years later when I eventually went into service I thought I was going to be very rich, but my savings book only had two shillings in it.

At assembly one morning Miss Pugh told the whole school that she was pleased to announce that the Council had chosen our school for the first School journey experiment. It was for the sixth form only and we were asked to speak to our parents about it if we would like to

67

go. We would have to bring in one shilling a week for the next 28 weeks towards the cost. The Isle of Wight was the location and the trip would be the last two weeks in June that year. It was 1931. We 'home' girls listened and thought how lovely it all sounded and were very disappointed that, of course, we would not be going. However we all started studies of the island in class, looking at its history and geography.

One Friday evening, some time later at the end of June, all eight of us from the sixth form were sent for by Mrs Jacobs. She told us that our school had asked the Committee if we could go to the Isle of Wight with the class and they had agreed. We would be going the next morning. Oh! What excitement. Mrs Jacobs added that she did not approve of some children having more privileges than others. We were sent to the needleroom to check and collect our cases, to have a bath and head wash and then to the Sick Bay to be examined by Nurse Saunders. Nurse Saunders was as excited and pleased as we were and gave us tuppence each. The next morning when we were all ready, we were sent to the Matron's house where she wished us a happy holiday and gave us a shilling each. My, we were rich!

We had a lovely, interesting holiday. There were 24 girls and four teachers; Miss Parker, Miss Bosher and Mr and Mrs Gloucester. Most mornings we went for a swim before breakfast. I had been paddling in the sea before but had never swam in it. I was surprised to find that it was much easier than swimming in the baths at school. During the day we went to places of interest, like Carisbrook Castle and Osbourne House, taking notes and making sketches in our notebooks. In the evenings we sat around a camp fire and sang songs. Apart from making our beds and tidying ourselves up, we had no work to do.

While I was on holiday I received a letter. It was the first time I had received an unopened letter. It had first been sent to the Children's House and the address had been crossed out and forwarded to me. I was very excited and wondered who could have written to me. When I tore it open I was pleased to see it was from Eva. She began the letter, *Dear Little Sister,* and wrote how lucky I was to be on the first School journey and hoped that I was being good. Then a bombshell. She told me that Mother had returned to St John's Road Institute and was very upset about it. She included Mother's address and asked me to send her a picture card to cheer her up. After I had finished reading, I felt stunned. What had happened? I had thought that Eva was looking after Mother. I cannot explain why, but I felt that something awful had happened. I had not noticed that the other girls had left the dormitory and I just sat on my bed staring into space. Mrs Gloucester came up to see why I had not gone down for breakfast. I showed her the letter and she read it. She told me that there was nothing to worry about as she felt sure that if Mother was ill then she would be taken care of. She did not know that I knew what sort of a place St John's Institute was. I asked her if I could be excused the outing that day and she left me upstairs. One of the girls brought me up some breakfast, but I could not touch it.

Later, when the others had gone out, Miss Parker came to see me. I told her that Mother was in the Workhouse again and that Eva had told me that they were very bad places. I fell into uncontrolled sobbing. Miss Parker left me and said she would come back when I had washed my face and calmed down. She returned a little later with a hot cup of sweet tea and she took me out into the garden. She told me that she knew my mother when she was teaching at St Mary's when Mother was about nine years old. She had been a rather boisterous, wayward girl but had been well liked because she was always so willing and cheerful. Miss Parker thought that this might have been her downfall in adult life. She explained to me that babies are not able to choose their parents, or say what circumstances they are born into. I asked her why I only had a mother and not a father. She told me that, of course, I did have a father it was just that my mother did not marry him. She added that while we were on the subject I ought to hear the truth about myself.

We went inside and into the sitting room to find a dictionary. She looked up the word 'illegitimate' and asked me to write it down along with the meaning of the word. She said that being born out of wedlock was no crime and that my mother was not a bad woman. She said that she was honest and hard working, but unfortunately also weak and self indulgent. She also said that Mother needed Eva and me to help and support her and that was the reason she wanted me to be fostered, so that at fourteen years I would go out to work for her. Miss Parker said that she was telling me all this to prepare me for the world outside and the people I would meet. Because of my illegitimacy she felt that people might be unkind and think I was from a bad home and she said that some families would not even let their children marry an illegitimate child. I wanted to ask Miss Parker more questions about Mother as there was so much more I wanted to know, but she told me to ask Auntie Ethel as she would be able to tell me more accurately what happened. She advised me not to tell people about being illegitimate, especially when I became an adult, as she felt that people often judged and blamed you for what had happened before your birth. She told me to tear up the piece of paper I had written on and forget about it and only to be truthful about my illegitimacy when signing official papers. She then told me not to waste any more tears over Mother, but to be brave and accept the situation.

A little later we had a mid-morning drink of lemonade and went into the village to the Post Office. This was my first experience of buying cards and stamps. I bought three of each; one for Eva, Matron and Mother. I wrote on them that I was having a lovely time and that I thought that the Isle of Wight was beautiful.

I never did find out why Mother was in the workhouse again.

Two days after returning to London, I received another letter from Eva. This time it had already been opened and inside were two birthday cards. On one card she wished me a 'happy birthday' and the other card was addressed to herself. Eva's birthday was one week after mine, it was her twenty-first birthday. Poor Eva, this card was the only one she received.

There were just two weeks more to the end of my very last term at school. All of us 'home' girls were sad at leaving school but we knew it had to be. I was dreading becoming a House girl and wondered what department I would be sent to work in. We wondered what we were going to do to break the drudgery of housework and looking after children. At least it would soon be the summer holidays with

Dover Court Bay to look forward to.

On the first Monday after breaking up from school, all eight of us were sent for by Miss Parsley to be told about our new duties. First of all we were shown into a large room surrounded by cupboards, each one numbered. The cupboards each contained a broom, dustpan and brush, feather duster, bucket with floor cloth, scrubbing brush and a hussif. The hussif contained dusters, tins of metal polish, one of floor polish, hearthstone, black lead and cleaning brushes. Each article was marked with the same number as the cupboard. My number was five. We were told that we were responsible for the cleanliness of our cupboards and that we were to wash the brooms and dusters once a week on Saturday morning. We then went into the Needleroom to receive our uniforms. We were each given a plain blue, short sleeved cotton frock with three white aprons to wear in the mornings and a hessian apron to use when scrubbing floors. For the afternoons we were given a plain brown cotton frock with long sleeves and three white afternoon aprons. Maud was given three very pretty lacy coffee coloured aprons, so we knew then that she would be working in the Matron's house.

Then a bombshell. Miss Parsley told us that the London County Council had been very wasteful in spending too much money on us and that everybody had got to cut back. This meant that the infants would not be going to Dover Court Bay and all eight of us had got to stay behind to look after them and do the housework. We were shocked and very disappointed. I felt sorry for the infants as I remembered my first paddle in the big sea as an infant, following Eva's footsteps in the water because I was afraid of the crabs. However, we actually had a really lovely time for the two weeks we spent with the infants. Their Officers had gone to Dover Court with the older children and we were left in the care of Officer Ridgeway, his wife and the domestic staff. There were thirty-five children between the ages of six and seven and a half years of age to look after but no very young ones as the Receiving Homes had been closed for about a year. This made it easier for us. The cook and the domestic staff spoilt us a little and sometimes gave us dripping toast for breakfast and jam on our bread for tea.

One day the domestic staff treated us all to a day's outing, we were taken by charabanc to Hampstead Heath and to the fair in the Vale of Health. It was a great day. We had a packed lunch of a bun, an apple and a penny bar of chocolate. We had rides on the swings and roundabouts. We slid down the Helter Skelter and even tried out our skill on the coconut shies. The infants had rides on the donkeys and were taken for rides round the fair in horse drawn gypsy caravans. It all ended too quickly, but it was great. When I went to bed that night, I though how kind the domestics were to take us and how it must have cost them a lot of pennies.

On Saturday afternoon, two weeks later, while playing with the children in the playground, I heard our band in the distance and they were playing a new tune. I was delighted and suddenly realised how much I had missed their music. We got very excited and decided to take the infants up to the lodge to meet the children coming back from Dover Court. When the gates opened and we saw our band boys with the lovely brass instruments, we clapped and cheered and joined them marching down the drive. We were all so happy. However, sadly our excitement was frowned upon and all eight of us were sent to Matron's office. She told us that we had behaved very badly as it was not done to show our emotions in such a way. It was not a good example to the other children, especially as we were now house girls. That night after we had put the infants to bed we were ordered by Matron to the dining hall to wash up the tea things from the whole school, and to clear the tables and re-lay them for breakfast. Luckily we were on good terms with the kitchen staff and they helped us as much as they dared. They gave us each an egg sandwich and a mug of milk before we went to bed. It was 10pm before we went to the dormitories that night. I had never been up so late before.

Christening, Confirmation and Preparing for Service

The next day, I was told that I would be looking after the women Officers' mess and their bedrooms. I knew that from now on, I was going to be kept very busy all day and every day.

There were five women Officers, two from the infant's department and three from the girl's. For a few days I worked with another girl, Rose, who was leaving soon as she was going into service. Rose told me that she had been for two interviews but did not know which one Matron had chosen for her. She said that Matron never walked with you, when she took you to an interview, but always went in front. Also, she did not sit with you in the bus, you had to sit behind her so that you could see when she got up to get off. Rose told me that when they arrived at one of the houses, she was sent round to the back door and Matron entered by the front. The Mistress had hardly spoken to Rose, only asking two questions; 'Are you an early riser?' and 'Are you a good worker?' Matron had replied that *all* her girls were well behaved and good workers and they were all sent with a smart maid's uniform. Rose was hoping that she would not be going to one of the places she went to see because Daisy had been sent to work there and had run away and when Daisy was sent back to us, she was a different person altogether.

Rose gave me a few tips on my new duties. She told me to try and ignore the Officers' requests for more food to be sent to the mess and not to go to the laundry to ask for their outdoor dresses to be sent back earlier. She explained that this would make me unpopular with the other staff and house girls. Also, she told me to always knock on Miss Hassell's bedroom door or anywhere that she might be, as she often had Mr. Ridgeway with her.

'What!' I said. 'What do they do then?'

'Oh' said Rose, 'they are sometimes kissing and cuddling.'

I was disgusted and said that I had my bottom smacked when I was seven years old for only winking at the boys. I even got my ears boxed when working with the infants for teaching five year old Ada how to kiss. I had noticed that Ada appeared not to be able to purse her lips to kiss and she never returned cuddles but just stayed still. It took her ages to even smile, so I had taken her in hand and tried to show her that I loved her. I think all of us helpers had a special little one we cared for. It might have been because we all needed someone to love.

When Rose left to go into service, I found that I was kept very busy all day, at the beck and call of the five Officers. I started work as usual at 6am. I began by clearing up the dirty cups and newspapers in the messroom and pushing the chairs away from the fireplace. Before I cleaned the grate, I put my hearthstone into a pail of warm water, it made it easier to use when soft. Then I put metal polish on the fender, to polish off when dry, and put some sticks of firewood into the furniture polish, in the hope that they would catch alight quicker. (These were tips from Rose.) I would then clean the fireplace, light the fire, do the hearth and polishing, sweep the room, lay the table for breakfast, and then run to the kitchen to make toast, which was done with a toasting fork in front of the bars of the kitchen ovens. Then I would carry the breakfast across the yard to the mess, put the kettle on the gas ring and have my own breakfast at 7.10am. After this, I would clear the staff breakfast things, sweep and dust the room, go upstairs and make the Officers' beds and tidy the rooms. I would turn out one room each day. Next I would clean the bath and toilet and wash the floor, making sure that there was enough toilet paper. For this we used old notebooks or outdated telephone directories from the Council Offices. Then back downstairs to lay the messroom table for dinner, for which there were two sittings; three Officers for twelve o'clock meal and the other two had theirs at one. I had to wait at the table, running backwards and forwards as I could not manage to carry all the dishes at once as they were large and heavy. After I had had my own dinner, I would clear the table and lay it for the second sitting. I then washed up everything and laid the table ready for the Officers' tea. I usually finished by 2pm. I then had to go and change my dress and put on my afternoon uniform and go in to domestic training classes.

On Mondays, I worked in the Laundry, mostly on the large wooden wringers. I put sheets through the rollers then folded them in half and placed them onto the hot pipes. I worked there until tea at 5pm. After tea I would go back to the Messroom and do any washing up there might be and lay the table for supper. In between, I would have to keep the fire burning and take the coal scuttle round to the boiler house for more coal. The boys had usually filled the coal buckets in the mornings and evenings, but it was seldom enough. I usually finished work after I had washed up the supper things at 7.30pm. However, the evenings were nearly always taken up with something, either drill or *Band of Hope.*

On Tuesday afternoons I was free and allowed out if I wished to go, although I had to be back by 5pm. On Wednesday afternoons I worked in the Kitchen, usually stoning raisins or making horseradish sauce, a horrible job which made my eyes water terribly. It was back to the Laundry on Thursday to iron our own uniform dresses and aprons. On Friday one of the Schoolrooms had to be cleaned for four of our girls to do their homework in. I was so proud of them as they were the first girls from St. Mary's at the secondary school to gain scholarships and two of them I remembered as babies when I was at the receiving home.

I had to help scrub the Playroom floor on a Friday night, each house girl scrubbed a strip of floor from one side of the room to the other. I found the scrubbing brush very large and cumbersome and the floor cloth was too big for me to wring out tightly. So I was nearly always the last to finish, often leaving the floor very wet.

There was no turning out of rooms on a Saturday, just cleaning cupboards and utensils. I would take my hussif to the supervisor in the laundry to have it replenished and she would also inspect the cupboards.

Sunday was a lovely day, not because it was a holy day but because there was no rush, and there were not so many staff on duty so there was less for me to do. I did not mind the church service although our Vicar was a bit boring. I never really understood his sermons and I think that he preached mainly to the staff. He did not know any of our names and apart from his sermons, he never spoke to us. I used to particularly enjoy the hymn singing, especially as our band used to play for us. Our Vicar was seldom away, but when he was, we had visiting Vicars. I can remember Rev. Dick Sheppard came to speak to us one Sunday and he stayed all day. He visited the Sunday School and came to talk at our Bible class. He told us about his work in Canterbury where he was a Dean and said that he had worked in St. Martin-In-The-Field. I asked him if this church was in the country as it was surrounded by fields. He explained that it was in the centre of London and then turned to our teacher, Miss Parker, asking her if it were possible to take us to see St. Martin-In-The-Field and St. Paul's Cathedral. Later that day he came into the dining hall while we were at tea and spoke to many of us. Alice told him that her father was in hospital and she had not seen him for a long time. The next week Alice was taken to see her father in hospital. I have always remembered this man's visit because he was so kind and understanding.

When Eva next came to visit me on 'old girls' Sunday, I told her that we now got Tuesday afternoons free. She thought we were very lucky and said that it did not happen in her day. She told me that she would be staying with Auntie Ethel for a few days as she had got a week's holiday. She asked me if my friends and I, would like to go out with her and we of course said yes.

The following Tuesday Minnie, Ada, Maud and I went up the drive and met Eva outside the gates. She took us to Wedmore Street where Auntie Ethel lived. Auntie Ethel now had seven children; Phyllis, the baby Auntie was keeping warm in the box when I visited before, was eight years old. And there was a new baby, Peter, in a pram in the garden and I was allowed to feed him with his bottle. Their home seemed so happy, cosy and warm and we had a lovely afternoon. I asked Auntie Ethel if I could bring my friends again and she said yes, but only one next time. So for many weeks on a Tuesday, I took a friend with me to Auntie Ethel's and everything seemed to be alright. Then one Tuesday, Auntie came to the door looking very pale and miserable. She said that she was surprised to see me because she had sent me a letter telling me not to come. She said that Phyllis and Elsie had got scarlet fever and were at St. Anne's, the fever hospital. The others were not allowed to go to school because of the infection. Auntie asked me if we would get into trouble for coming, but I said that I did not think so. We had only been told to stay away from Caledonian Market and not to go too far away. As we walked home I wondered why I had not received the letter. I knew that it would have been opened and read before I received it and surely, if Auntie thought it best to stop us visiting her, the Matron would have thought the same. When we arrived at the side gate, Mr. Ridgeway was there to meet us and ordered us to go to Matron's office immediately. As soon as we were in front of Matron, she shouted at us saying 'Where have been this afternoon?'

I told her that we had been to see my Auntie Ethel in Holloway Road.

'Who gave you permission?' she asked and I replied,

'Nobody.'

She then asked why I had not told the Officer on gate duty where we were going. Ada and I told her that the gate was open and nobody was in the Lodge. I said that often there was nobody in the Lodge when we went out, and when there was, we had never been asked where were going. Matron then rang the bell and asked Clare to fetch Mr. Jacobs and Mr. Ridgeway. When they arrived, Matron told them that Ada and I had broken the rules by visiting relatives, and that we had done it every Tuesday. She also told him that we had said that there was seldom anyone on duty at the Lodge when we were going out. Mr. Ridgeway denied this. He said that he saw us out every week and had not asked us where we were going because he thought that we knew the rules. Matron dismissed us and said that we were lucky not to receive a good caning. Consequently, we had our pocket money stopped and were not allowed out for a month afterwards.

Two days after this episode, Minnie and I were in the dining hall putting out bread for tea when Miss Hassell entered from the Matron's house. She looked very red in the face and cross. We had not seen her since we went out on that Tuesday as she had been off duty. Miss Hassell wanted us to go immediately to get our baths as she was going to be busy that evening with new admissions. I went first and Minnie said that she would soon catch me up.

Just as I was getting out of the bath and reaching for a towel, Miss Hassell came in and said, 'I will not have you telling lies about me.' She forced me over the side of the bath and thrashed me with a brush. It seemed to go on for a long time. I tried to get up from the bath after she stamped out and slammed the door, but I fell on the stone floor as it was very slippery and wet. Minnie came in and tried to help me get up but I could not stand, so she went away and came back with Miss Chaff who wrapped me in a bath towel and carried me over to the Sick Bay.

The next morning when I woke up, my left eye was bandaged and Nurse Saunders was washing me. She said, 'I had to send for Doctor last night and Matron is not very pleased about it.' The Doctor came back to see me and was quite jovial, he asked me how I fell to get such a beautiful black eye. He then turned to Nurse Saunders and said,

'She is not one of our usual ones. She is not a naughty or difficult child is she?'

At that moment Matron came into the ward.

'Well', she said to me, 'How did it happen?'

I did not answer. What could I say? Then she said to Doctor,

'She is a child that does not speak the truth, I think she asked for what she got.' Doctor spoke to Nurse Saunders then all three of them left. When Doctor, Matron and Nurse came back into the ward they were followed by Miss Hassell. I am not quite sure what happened but it was as though the blood had gone from my head, I felt giddy and terribly cold. Then everything blacked out.

I was in the Sick Bay for quite a while. My friends were allowed to visit me on Tuesday afternoons and Miss Parker came in on Sundays. One Sunday she brought Eva with her. Eva had not been told that I was in the Sick Bay so I explained to her what had happened. Miss Parker was very surprised as she had been told that I had had an accident. Miss Parker gave me a little cuddle and Eva kissed me and said,

'Please darling, do try and be good. You are a big girl now. So don't get into any more trouble.'

Eva asked Nurse Saunders why I had been in the Sick Bay for so long if I had only had a punishment. And Nurse Saunders replied that the difficulty was, nobody could make up their minds as to where I should work. Doctor had said that I was to have light work and that I was not to come into contact with Miss Hassell. They then realized that they were all talking in front of me, said their farewells and left. A few days after this I started helping the house girls in the kitchen and taking meals to the patients. Then Nurse Saunders asked me if I would like to work in the Sick Bay. I was pleased because most of the house girls liked working there.

There were three house girls working in the Sick Bay, myself, Charlotte and Lillian. Charlotte was a very jolly, rather stout girl of about 16 years of age. She had been transferred to us from Putney Childrens' Home and attended a special school. Her trouble was that she had difficulty in reading, she got all of the words backwards. So if she had a letter we would read it for her, together with any notices on the board. Charlotte had already been for two job interviews; one as a laundress in a Girls' boarding school which she thought she would like as she enjoyed ironing. Shortly after I started work at the Sick Bay Charlotte left and I hoped that she got the job in the laundry.

Lillian was a very tall pale girl with fair, almost white hair and large grey eyes. She took life very seriously and was clever at school. She had been with us for a long time, coming from the Soldiers and Sailors Orphanage. I believe her father had been killed in the Great War.

For a month Lillian was working in the Sick Bay kitchen. We were both up at 5.30am with the other house girls and started work at 6am. Lillian looked after the kitchen stove and kept the kitchen clean, she cooked the porridge for the children and laid trays for their breakfast. Then she washed up after the meals and was responsible For a month Lillian was working in the Sick Bay kitchen. We were both up at 5.30am with the other house girls for cleaning the receiving room, the treatment room floor, the corridors and the front hall. After each month, we changed over duties.

For my first month in the Sick Bay, I looked after the Nurses' sitting room and bedrooms. The work was similar to what I had been doing for the other Officers, except that there were only two resident nurses. Work was much easier as not only were there less people to look after, but the rooms were smaller. I was also responsible for the staff bathroom and toilet, together with the dusting and polishing of the upstairs landing and stairs.

I had thought that working in the Sick Bay would be very quiet and dull but far from it. There were always people visiting. There were the children who needed treatment or dressings, deliveries of bread, the boys fetching coal, the office porter with letters and Matron coming to see patients every morning at 9am. We were told to stay out of her way and never to disturb the nurses while they were with Matron or Doctor. However, this did not worry Lillian or me as we were so used to being ignored. Many a time I had had an officer step over me while I was scrubbing or polishing the floors. There were also two women who came in daily to clean the front and back doorsteps and to clean the wards, and even they were expected to keep away while Matron was about. They told me that Matron never spoke to them either. When Matron left it was usually time for the nurses' mid-morning drink. The nurses allowed Lillian and me to make ourselves some tea and have a biscuit, and even a piece of cake sometimes. They often chatted to us when they had time. This was unusual for me as I had seldom chatted to adults and, at first, I was 'dumbstruck'.

One Sunday morning at the Church service, after the Vicar had given his sermon, he read out some names from a list. Ada's, Minnie's and mine were among them, but not Maud's. He said that we would be christened the following week. We were very surprised. We all thought that we had been christened already because we had got a name. When I told Nurse Saunders about it, she was delighted and said that it was a wonderful experience. She explained that every child in the Home had to be brought up into the religion of the Church of England. The Church had certain rules, one of them being that you had to be confirmed to establish your faith and to secure your membership in the Church. We asked why Maud was not going to be christened and were told that she must have been christened before she came to the receiving home, but she would join us in confirmation.

The following Sunday morning, Nurse Saunders asked me to fetch

Minnie and Ada. When we were all together, she brushed our hair, tied on a bow then gave us each a little book of the New Testament. The books had white leather covers with little silver crosses embossed on them. This was a wonderful act of generosity and made us feel very special. We went into the Dining Hall for the service with all the children to be christened sitting in the two front rows, the girls in front of the boys. Half way through the service when all the prayers and psalms had been sung, our Vicar came up to us with a small bowl of water in his hand. He went along the line asking each of us for our name, made a small wet cross on our foreheads, mumbled back our names, said a prayer, then went on to the next child. When we came away from the Hall Minnie asked me many questions about the service but I could not answer. I very rarely took any interest in the Church service as to me church was just a routine thing. It was merely a time when I did not have to work, although I enjoyed hearing the band playing and singing the hymns.

One Tuesday evening after our christening we were told to go to the classroom in the infants' department. This was to learn the catechism to prepare us for confirmation. Our Vicar read the catechism to us then expected us to learn it parrot fashion. It was all questions and answers and I honestly did not understand it. I could not accept to honour my mother and father, as I really did wonder what they had done for me. However the Vicar told us not to question these things but to accept them.

Some months later all the girls that had taken confirmation classes went to be confirmed at St Mary's Church in Highbury. When we arrived there were a lot of other children all waiting to be confirmed. The girls were wearing white dresses and ribbons with white shoes and socks and the boys looked very smart in white shirts. These children were sitting in the middle front pews and we sat behind them. Our boys did not come with us as they had been confirmed three months earlier. It was a lovely service. The choir boys sang beautifully. One thing puzzled us though, half way through the service a silver plate was passed round and I looked over the shoulder of the girl in front of me and saw her put a penny on the plate. We didn't have one

81

penny between the nine of us as we had not had any pocket money for ages so we were unable to put any money in the collection. However I came away from the church feeling happy, thinking that now I would try and be a good Christian. The following Sunday, we all got up very early as we had to walk to Highbury for our first Holy Communion at 6.30am. We received our first sacrament and this time I came away from church not feeling so happy. I was afraid that if I did anything wrong Jesus would be cross and punish me. When I saw Miss Parker that afternoon she dismissed my fears and said that the Christian faith was to help us lead a better life, not to frighten us. Then she told us that she had at last got Matron's permission to take us to London to see St. Martin-In-The-Fields and St. Paul's Cathedral as suggested by the Rev Dick Sheppard.

The following Tuesday we took an open topped red bus and went all the way to the City. This was the first time that I had ever been on a bus and we were allowed to go upstairs. I could see the streets from above, over garden fences, fancy chimneys and decorative roofs. To me this was wonderful and I thought London a lovely place. Mrs Gloucester came with us as well. She and Miss Parker were still teachers. They told us about Wren, his architecture and the history of the Churches and asked us to write an essay on what we had seen and learnt. This was to be an opening to other outings. These two lovely people, in their own time, also took us to visit Kew Gardens, the London Zoological Gardens and took us on a river bus to Greenwich.

Interviews and Chosen for Service

It was 1932 and my birthday. I was fifteen years of age. I received a card from Eva in the post and was given one from Nurse Saunders. When she wished me a 'Happy Birthday' she told me that Maud was going out that afternoon with Matron for an interview. I felt a bit down, as I knew that I would be going soon too. I just hated changes. I suppose I must have been very insecure, as I did not like meeting new people or doing anything new. I always liked to be told about them first and hated it when they came suddenly.

With St. Mary's soon to be closed Matron was getting worried about us girls being undersized and underweight because we could not stay on at the home. Nurse Lloyd was ordered to weigh us every fortnight. I was given a medicine called *Parishes Food* and extra milk at breakfast time. Dr Jenkins had ordered this for several of us because he said we were underweight. St. Mary's continued to get smaller. The infants had all reached the age of seven or over and a lot of them had been transferred to other children's' homes away in the country. Officers Jackson and Hassell had gone with them. I hoped that there was somebody to stop Officer Hassell from being such a big bully. I had once heard her saying with glee, 'I am going to give a good spanking to six of them tonight as I caught them spitting at one another in the playroom.'
I was sorry that Officer Bishop had not gone away with them as well.

During this time, on one Saturday afternoon, all of us house girls were told to scrub out all of the cupboards in the infants' department. We were surprised at the number of cupboards full of books. They must have been left behind from when Maxwell House was a school. The following week we went to their dormitory and washed down the iron bedsteads and some men came and took them away in a portage. With the House closed and no noise from the little ones, it seemed very quiet and spooky.

One day Minnie and I went with Matron for an interview in Billingsgate. Minnie was full of fun, she was able to mimic Matron's walk to a 'T', with her nose up in the air, walking as though she did not own us. I was in fits of laughter and Matron turned and told me to stop 'that vulgar giggling.' We went to a flat that was built on top of the wharf where there was a very strong smell of fish. We were met by a very little elderly lady. Minnie and I were told to sit in the kitchen while she spoke to Matron in the sitting room. We joined them later. She did not ask us to sit down. She told us that she was looking for someone to take complete care of the flat, to do the housework, laundry and cooking for her and her husband. She told us that her husband was a superintendent at Billingsgate Market and she would pay seven shillings and sixpence a week. When we got back on the bus we sat well back so that Matron could not hear us. Minnie said that she would like to work there. She thought that the place was much smaller than she was used to and she liked it because you could see the River Thames from the kitchen windows. I told her that I did not like the smell of fish. When we followed Matron off the bus, she turned and said 'Don't let the smell of the fish worry you, you will soon get used to it.'

A few weeks after this Nurse Saunders found out that Matron had heard from the Billingsgate lady and told us that she had chosen Minnie to work for her.

I went for another interview, this time with Ada. It was in Highgate, in a very large house. Matron arrived at the house first, went up the steps and rang the bell. When the door was opened to her she told us to hurry up and go round the back of the house. As we were about to do so, a man in a livery beckoned for us to come up to the door. When we got into the house he explained that the back door was through the garden gate and that we would not be able to find it. He showed us all into a library and asked us to sit down. Matron did not speak while we waited. A very stern looking lady came in. She was of medium height with short black hair, greying at the sides. She said to Matron, 'Ah! So these are the girls.'

Then she pulled a silk cord by the fireplace and in came a motherly looking lady whom she called 'Anderson.' She asked her to take us girls and show us around the house while she talked to Matron. Anderson was a very nice chatty person with blue twinkling eyes. She told Ada and me that she was the Housekeeper and that her husband was the chauffeur and gardener. She said that she had worked for the family since she was fourteen years old. She had met her husband when he delivered meat to the house. He then got a job as gardener and houseboy. They got married in 1912 and had worked together at the house ever since. Then Anderson told us that Miss Hilda, the mistress, was looking for a companion for her sister, Miss Edith. Miss Edith was a semi-invalid who needed somebody willing and cheerful to be with her most of the time. When we arrived back in the kitchen, Matron and Miss Hilda were there waiting. Miss Hilda said to us,

'Do you like the house?' and 'What do you think of the bedroom?' We both said that we thought the house was very large, but very nice. Ada said that the bedroom was pretty. Then Miss Hilda said,

'Come and join your Matron in the drawing room for tea.'
As I looked up to reply I saw Matron's face. She looked shocked at the thought of having tea with us. Whether Miss Hilda had noticed or Matron had said anything, I did not know, but Anderson gave us our tea in the kitchen. However, when Miss Hilda came in, she winked at us before returning to Matron. Both Ada and I enjoyed the afternoon. It was not like being interviewed, more like an afternoon outing. Neither of us expected to go there to work.

Two days later I went on another interview, this time there were three of us, Ada, Jean and myself. Jean used to wear splints as she had something wrong with the bones of her leg. She had been in hospital for a long time but now it was better and she only had a slight limp. This time we went to a big private boarding school, set in its own grounds in Chalk Farm. We were shown around the building and when we arrived at the Laundry our friend, Charlotte, spotted us. She waved and coo-eed. Matron looked at her very crossly and forbade us to answer. In the Kitchen there was another girl that had left St. Mary's about three years before. Her name was Flossie and she had started as a kitchen maid, and was now an assistant cook. Matron knew the person who was showing us around very well as quite a few of our girls had gone there. I thought that it would be nice to work there because

I would know somebody.

After each interview I would tell Nurse Saunders all about them. That evening I told her that I would like to go to the girls' boarding school because I knew two of the domestics there. Nurse Saunders told me that if I was going to make a break then I ought to make a clean break and meet entirely new people. However, she said

'It is disappointing that you do not get a choice.'

She said that neither Ada nor I could go yet anyway, as we were not up to five stone in weight and that Dr Jenkins would not let us go until we were the correct weight. Then she said,

'I do not know what we are going to do with little Ada, she'll never be able to do domestic work.'

I told her that Ada did beautiful needlework and had embroidered a lovely table centre for Miss Parsley and she could also use a sewing machine.

'I didn't know that' said Nurse, 'perhaps something will turn up along that line.'

One day I got a message to say that I was wanted at the Lodge. At that time we were getting sent all over the place because there were only six of us house girls left. As I walked along the drive I saw that terrible green van parked near the visiting room and my heart almost stopped. I wanted to run away. I had not seen Mother, or asked about her, for such a long time and I felt I was just not ready to see her again. As I went into the room I did not see her at first among the other women and children. Then she appeared from nowhere, put her arms about me and gave me one of her tight squeezes. I did not kiss her and I just waited for her to release me. When she did and I was able to look at her properly, I realised how worn and tired she looked. He eyes were red and her face was damp. She had been crying and my heart softened a little. I asked her what had happened to her, and with this Mother did cry. She said,

'I'm sorry to have let you and Eva down.'

She told me that Eva did not come and see her anymore and she hoped that I would visit when I left. She then asked me to help her to get out of the workhouse by sponsoring her. I did not know what sponsoring meant and did not know what to say. I was a bit dazed and wished that Eva was with me. Mr Ridgeway came over to Mother and told her that a Welfare Officer wanted to talk to us both, so Mother and I went into the Lodge where there was a gentleman sitting at the desk with some notes in front of him. He told Mother,

'I am here to tell you that your daughter will be leaving this home soon and will be placed in a suitable household where she will earn her living and receive food and shelter. Have you any objections?' Mother asked if they had found me a job yet. The Welfare man replied,

'No, we have not found her one yet. You see she is small for her age, so it is difficult to place her.'
Mother suddenly came to life and said, 'Well, that's because you've half starved her.' Then she got abusive, saying that I ought to have been fostered a long time ago and that she did not want me to be a servant girl.

'Stop this silly behaviour' said the man, 'or else I will put an order on you to stop all privileges.'
I felt awful. I wished I had never been there. I squeezed Mother's hand, waved my goodbye and started to leave. As I got to the door Mother shouted after me,

'Never mind girl, I'll speak up for you, I won't let them send you away.'
This did not worry me very much as I was more concerned that Mother did not look at all well. I felt sure that she was ill. I ran as fast as I could down the drive. I did not want to hear the whistle or see all those funnily dressed ladies get into the van. As I was passing the Matron's house, Mrs Jacobs put her head out of the window and said,

'Stop running. You are a young lady now, ladies never run.'
One morning, as I was making the toast for the nurses' breakfast, Nurse Lloyd said that I was to see Doctor Jenkins at 10am and that she would like to weigh me before I saw him. I told Ada this on my way to the dining room and she said she already knew as she and Jean were also to have a medical that morning. When Doctor saw me, he was very friendly and jovial. Nurse Saunders told him that I was to be

87

discharged soon and he asked what sort of a post it was. Nurse replied that it was a large household, with a housekeeper and a chauffeur and she thought I was going there as a housemaid. My heart sank. I had so much wanted to go to the girls' boarding school. Doctor said that the post sounded all right for me, checked me over and then dismissed me. I asked Nurse Saunders whether Jean had got the job at the girls' school. Nurse told me that she had. They had felt that work in a school would be heavier than in a private house, and that Jean could manage it better than me.

Some days later Matron brought a lady visitor into the dining hall while we were having tea. She looked extremely smart, wearing a straight navy blue tailored costume with a white blouse, a cloche hat and black high heeled shoes. It took me some minutes before I recognised her as the lady I went to see in Highgate with Ada. As we were marching out of the dining hall, I was told to go to Matron's office.

'Here's the young rascal,' said Matron as she again introduced me to Miss Hilda.

I was very surprised at Matron's pleasantness. Miss Hilda shook my hand and said,

'I thought that I would like to see you again before you come to live with us.'

She told me that Matron had said I was cheerful and easy to get on with, and she felt that I would be just the right person to be a companion to her sister, Miss Edith. She explained that Miss Edith was unable to get about and spent most of the day in a bathchair. She had a nurse to see to her requirements, to get her up in the mornings and help her to bed in the evening. I would be required to spend most of the day with Miss Edith as she needed someone within calling distance of her all the time, to sit with her sometimes and to keep her company. Miss Hilda then asked me what I thought and whether I would like to do that. I did not know what to say as I had so wanted to go to the boarding school where I knew two of the girls. However, Miss Hilda went on talking. She explained that Anderson, their housekeeper, was getting on in years and was unable to be with Miss Edith as much as she would like. She told me Matron had brought six of us girls to see them and I was the one she and Anderson chose. She then said,

'Please say that you will come, we both want you.'

Had I heard right? I was unsure whether she meant it. I looked up into Miss Hilda's face and saw she was smiling. I felt so excited that somebody at last had said that they wanted me, I did not know what to say. I wanted to reach up and kiss her. I realised that Matron was watching me expectantly.

'Well,' she said, 'speak up, where's your tongue?'

I looked again at Miss Hilda and she gave me one of her naughty winks. I pulled myself together and said,

'Yes, please, Miss Hilda, I would love to come.'

'That's settled then,' she said, 'I'll tell Miss Edith all about you and I hope that you will be very happy with us.'

She then turned to Matron and asked how soon I could come, and Matron replied that I could be ready by Wednesday, in two days time. Miss Hilda told Matron that she would send William for me at 10am. Matron almost bowed her out of the front door and outside I saw William getting out of the car to meet Miss Hilda. As I walked back to the Sick Bay I felt wonderful, somehow I knew that everything was going to be all right. It was grand to feel wanted, I was walking on air.

When I arrived back, Nurse Saunders and Lloyd were having supper in the Kitchen and they invited me to sit down with them.

'Well, have you got a job?' asked Nurse Saunders.

I said yes and that I was going to the house where I had been for an interview in Highgate. I said that they had seen six of us and that she and her housekeeper had chosen me. I told them about my duties and Nurse Saunders warned me that there were sure to be some household duties as well. She asked me how much I was going to be paid and whether I would get a half day a week off. I had forgotten to ask these questions and felt a little worried but was sure Miss Hilda meant it when she said that she wanted me and hoped I would be very happy. Nurse Saunders told me not to worry and said she would discuss the subject the next morning with Matron.

When I went to bed that night I began to have more doubts; perhaps it was not right for me to go as a companion to an invalid lady; I knew how to do housework better and what was Miss Edith like? I hoped that she was not too irritable and impatient: Why could they not get someone older to be with her? With all these questions I found it difficult to sleep, but eventually dropped off.

The next morning Matron came into the Kitchen with Nurse Saunders while I was washing up. Straight away she went for me, telling me not to get high ideas about myself. She told me that I had been trained to serve and go into domestic service and that that would be my place in life. She asked if I had anything that I wanted to take with me. I said yes, that I had two books. She told me to take the books to Miss Parsley that morning and she would check my case with me in the evening. I took my book of *Parables from Nature*, and *Little Women*, both of which I had received at school as prizes. I remembered another book I had received as a prize when I was about nine years old. I had painted a picture of an old lady with a little girl for a competition run by the Manazawatee Tea Company. Two elderly gentlemen had given me a prize of a beautiful red book with gold lettering on the cover, called *The Big Book for Little People* by Arthur Mee. It was a lovely book, with lots of stories, pictures, games and puzzles and things to make in it. An Officer had told me that she would put the book away and keep it safe for me. I never saw it again. This happened to almost anything we had. We very seldom owned anything of our own.

When I went to the Needleroom later that evening, Matron was there with a brown fibre case opened in front of her.

'Come on,' she said, 'let's get this over quickly.'
She put aside new garments and said, 'Put these on tomorrow morning.'
Then she counted out three maid's morning dresses, six morning aprons, three maid's afternoon dresses, six afternoon aprons, two vests, two bodices, four pairs of black stockings, four pairs of knickers, one face flannel, a brush and comb and twelve diapers. The diapers looked like large face flannels to me, so I asked Matron why I needed so many. Answering me, she said,

'Oh, you will need a piece of elastic to tie them on.'
So she got a card of elastic and cut a piece off. Then she put in my two books and placed a Bible with them. She closed the case.

'That's all, now you will go to the Sick Bay as usual at 6am, then after breakfast get yourself ready and come to my office at 9.45am.'

That evening I went round the whole building to say goodbye to everybody, especially to see Cook and the Kitchen Domestic Officers. They had been so kind to all of us over the years, and I knew that I was going to miss them, especially Miss Chaff. I went to the dormitories, to see the little ones first, kissed and said goodnight to them all. That night, Ada and I talked for a long time. We wondered how Maud and Minnie were and all the others we had come here with. We had been told that Charlie had died of diphtheria a few years before and that Thomas was now the leader in the band. Ada told me that Matron was going to try and get her a job at Court, dressmaking. How I hoped that she would get it. I was lucky because I knew what job I was going to. I had even seen my Mistress again. I had no fears and I felt confident. I think that we eventually fell asleep talking.

The next morning I went to see Nurse Saunders before I left for breakfast. She told me that she had loved me since I was a tiny baby and she would always think of me and hoped that I would be a good girl and do well. She said that I had been brought to her from St. Mary's Hospital at eight weeks old, weighing only five pounds. She said that I was so tiny that they had to nurse me in the kitchen in a basket because that was the warmest place. She asked me to write to her and then gave me a little gift of a small black leather handbag. Inside the bag was a small purse with a florin in it. We cuddled and she kissed me saying,

'Please continue to say your prayers, *He* is your real friend.'
I promised that I would, then ran as fast as I could so as not to be late on my last day.

I waited in the hall outside Matron's office, but there was no-one about. Then at 10am the front door bell rang. It was William. Matron arrived hurriedly, saying that she had been held up and reminded me to come back and visit on Old Girl's Sunday. I asked if I might say goodbye to Mr Jacobs. She said that she did not think it necessary, but she was sure that he wished me well. She then opened the front door. William came and took the case, opened the car door for me, tied the case on the rack at the back of the car and without a word, drove off.

PART FOUR

A New Life

I arrived at Hillbreu House, Highgate, in time for lunch.

At last I met Miss Edith, who was not an old lady as I had imagined, but was about forty and very pretty. She told me that she needed somebody so badly because she hated to worry her dear sister who was a very busy lady, or Anderson because she was 'getting on'.

The day passed in a daze and later that first night at bedtime, as I knelt down to say my prayers, I thought of all the people who had been so good to me. I asked God to love and bless them, to take care of my special friends and to forgive my mother, even though I did not know if she had done anything wrong. I also thought of my teachers and I hoped I would see Miss Parker again so that I could thank her for all her love and kindness. When I stopped I found that I had been crying and as I wiped away my tears, I felt a sort of peace had come over me. I knelt in silence and in the dark for a long time. I thanked God for his love and asked him to make me worthy of it. When I eventually got into bed, I felt that life was good and that I was living in a great wide beautiful world.

It was very dark when I awoke the next morning. As I lay in bed, I wondered what I would be doing that day. What does a companion do? I asked myself. I thought that it would be better if I was a housemaid as I knew how to make beds and keep places clean. The house was very still and quiet and it was still dark. I tried to go to sleep again but was unable to. I longed to get up and put on my new maid's uniform. I had seen the cotton dress, it was a pretty colour of light mauve check material. I got so bored with waiting. Suddenly I could hear movements downstairs. The boiler was being raked and made up and I could also hear running water. At last somebody was up!

I jumped out of bed and went to the wall by the door to turn on the light switch but I was unable to reach it. So I very quietly opened the door and listened. I went downstairs, feeling my way by holding on to the banisters and when I got down to the hall I could see a light shining under the kitchen door. I went in and saw Martin pouring himself a cup of tea. When he saw me he looked very surprised.

'Hey, young Miss,' he said, 'you must not come in here. You've only got a nightie on, you will catch a death o' cold. Go back upstairs quickly, Anderson is just on her way to see you and will be cross at you running about like that.'

I told him that everywhere was very dark and that I was unable to turn on the lights, so he came into the hall with me and put the lights on and then called up to his wife.

'Maria, Maria, the little Miss is down here. I'm sending her back upstairs, she's freezing cold.'

When I had reached the first floor, Anderson was on the second floor looking over the banister.

'You naughty girl, you must not run about the house like that. You must put on your slippers and a dressing gown over your nightie.'

I told her that I had not got any slippers and had never had a dressing gown. Anderson appeared a little impatient and told me to get into bed and drink up the cup of tea she had brought me, while it was still hot.

'I hope that you take sugar as I have put some in. Now tuck down under the bedclothes and get warm and you are not to get dressed until I come to you at seven.'

It seemed hours later when Anderson came back to my room. She had with her an attaché case, which she placed on the bedside locker, opened and, from it, took out some really lovely undergarments. They were soft and silky in very pretty colours.

'Now you are not to put on the clothes that you brought with you. I will put out a set of these. What colour would your like?'

I told Anderson that everything that I had brought with me was new and they were the only things that I had been given for keeps from St. Mary's. If I did not wear them, what was I to do with them? Anderson ignored my question and she put out a blue set, telling me to put it on quickly.

'When you have dressed, go into the bathroom, wash your face and hands, then come downstairs when you hear the breakfast gong. I must go quickly because we have breakfast at 8.15, so don't be long.'

95

When Anderson had gone, I had another long look at the clothes that she had put out for me. They really were beautiful. I had never seen anything so soft and silky. There was a white vest made of wool and silk material. I put it on. Although it was so light, it felt warm. Much better, I thought, than my own flannelette vest. The other undies were trimmed with lace and were far too nice to be hidden by a dress. The dress was light blue in a fine wool material and was trimmed with a dark blue silk collar and cuffs. I looked at myself in the mirror. I could not believe it was me that I could see. I was so delighted, I could not stop looking at myself. I turned and twisted and tried to look at the back of myself. I curtsied and lifted up my skirt to show the lace edge of my petticoat. It was all so lovely, I could not believe that it was real. Surely I was having a wonderful dream.

The gong sounded very loudly and I came to. I quickly put on the black lace-up shoes I arrived in, rushed to the bathroom to wipe my face and then ran down the stairs as fast as I could. When I got downstairs Anderson said that she thought it was an elephant coming down the stairs, she had never heard such a noise. And why had I not tidied my hair? We went into a side room off the kitchen, called the Morning Room where Miss Hilda was already sitting at the table.

'Hello!' she said, 'I hope that you slept well.'

Then she said,

'We really must do something about your shoes, they will tear the carpets and scratch the parquet flooring. Perhaps Martin will take you and Anderson to the shops this afternoon. But now let us have Grace.'

I expected to hear somebody say it, but there was silence as we all just bowed our heads for about a minute. We then got up from the table and went to the sideboard to help ourselves to breakfast. There seemed to be an awful lot of food, but I just helped myself to some porridge (although I did not really want any) and managed to eat it. I was so excited I could not drink my cup of tea. After breakfast Miss Hilda said that she was leaving me in the good care of Anderson for the day because she unfortunately had to go out.

I helped Anderson clear the table and asked if I could wash up.

'Oh no,' she said, 'the housemaid Dorothy will do that. I expect she is in already making the beds upstairs.'

She asked me to bring down the clothes I wore the day before so Mrs. Woodward could wash, pack and send back them back to my school. I was astonished.

'No,' I said, 'you can't do that. They're mine and I would like to keep them.'

Anderson said,

'But they are mostly maid's uniforms and you will not be wearing them here and they are far too small for anyone else to wear.'

I asked if I could take the books out of the case.

'Of course you may,' said Anderson, and she gave me a little cuddle. 'Don't be upset. I will speak to Miss Hilda and see what we can do. Now, this morning I will take you upstairs to Miss Edith, she's looking forward to seeing you. Perhaps you could stay and have a chat with her. But first you must wait until nurse has gone, she comes in each day, except Sundays, to help Miss Edith wash and dress.'

Later that morning Anderson knocked on Miss Edith's door very gently. The nurse called out,

'Come in'

and as we went in she came towards the door and gave me a peculiar look. She said to Anderson,

'Oh! So this is her, I didn't think she would be so young.'

Miss Edith called,

'Come in, I have been looking forward to seeing you again. Did you sleep well?'

I said that I had. Then I stood silently by while she and Anderson chatted to one another. They seemed to go on for ages talking about how I should bide my time. Perhaps, they said, I might like to go for a walk or go into the garden or get a book to read. I felt so foolish just standing there. Obviously they had no idea what to do with me. Then Dorothy, the housemaid, put her head round the door and asked if she should pack my school case with the clothes. I spoke quickly, saying,

'No, thank you, I will put them away myself.'

Miss Edith told Anderson that she had better go with me. I think that they were afraid I was going to put them on. We went upstairs to my room. Dorothy had already made my bed.

The case with the silky clothes in it was still open on the bedside locker. Anderson told me to put the clothes in the second drawer down of the chest of drawers. She said that the top drawer was for gloves and hankies and the third drawer was for my nightclothes. Then she opened my school case and said that she would put in the clothes I wore yesterday, after Mrs. Woodward had washed and ironed them. She told me that Mrs. Woodward came in to do the laundry three days a week and also on those days she cleaned the front porch and polished the red steps up to the front door and she washed the bathroom, the kitchen and hall floors as well. Next Anderson told me that Dorothy was her and Martin's eldest daughter and she came in every day from 8.30am to 4.30pm to help generally around the house and also with the meals. As we went downstairs I asked her what I would be doing. She said,

'I will take you to Miss Edith, I think that she will want to chat with you for a bit. At 10.30 I will be making tea in the kitchen, so I will call you down and then you can come and meet us all.'

I knocked on Miss Edith's door, and as I went in she said,

'I'm glad that you came back to me, come and sit down and tell me about yourself.'

This rather puzzled me as there wasn't very much that I could say. She already knew where I had come from, my name and my age. What else could I tell her? I had sat for quite a few minutes in silence, wondering what on earth I could say when Miss Edith spoke.

'I have heard that you have a sister, would you like her to come and see you sometimes?'

I was delighted and at once told her that would be wonderful. This loosened my tongue and I talked for ages telling her about how wonderful my big sister was. I told her that Eva was seven years older than me, that she loved me very much and could only come to see me on some Sundays because she had so much work to do. Then I went on to tell her about Miss Parker and said that she was my favourite teacher, and then how Nurse Saunders had said that she had loved me since I was a baby. I went on and on about St. Mary's and she just listened, smiled and nodded until Dorothy came in with a tray of tea and biscuits for Miss Edith, and asked if she could take me downstairs for tea.

When we went into the kitchen, Anderson pointed to the chair beside her for me. She then introduced me to everyone. Firstly, to her husband Martin who, she told me, looked after the garden and car, and drove Miss Hilda to the City most mornings and Miss Edith for a ride sometimes in the afternoon. Then she introduced me to Mrs. Woodward who told me herself what her work was, and that there was also a laundry bag especially for my use. She said that she had worked at the house for fifteen years, and hoped to do fifteen more. She was a rough and ready but kindly soul, and was, I think about fifty years of age. She lived in the Holloway Road with her two grown-up sons who she wished would get married soon.

Anderson looked round for Dorothy, and then said with great pride, 'This is our eldest daughter, Dorothy.'

Dorothy was a big, rosy cheeked, buxom woman. She was busy at the cupboard getting her father's favourite digestive biscuits out. She put the biscuits on the table then sat down and grinned at me.

'Well,' she said, 'my mum was right, you are about half the size of my Jenny and she is the same age as you. We hope that you will like it here, there's not much to amuse an orphan girl like you.'

'Well, that will do,' said Anderson, 'I'm sure that once she gets settled in she'll have plenty to do.'

And with that she told me to return to Miss Edith, as they had to get on, and to come down for lunch at 12.30pm.

Miss Edith was sitting in a chair with a very long seat where she was able to stretch out her legs. The top part of the chair was like an armchair and underneath were three wheels, two under the seat and a smaller one under the feet. She asked me to wheel the 'chaise longue' over to the French window so that she could look out on to the balcony. I looked all around the room wondering what it was I had to move. After a moment or two I asked,

'What is a shayz long?'

Miss Edith laughed.

'Oh, you haven't seen a chair like this one before. Never mind, just push me over to the windows.'

Then she asked me to go to the library and get a book of my choice to read to her for a little while. I went running down the stairs making such a noise with my shoes that Anderson came out into the hall.

'Goodness gracious me child, why are you running about? What's the hurry?'

I told her that I had to go to the library and I was on my way to ask her where it was. She took me through the dining room into a small room where three walls were lined with bookcases full of books. I told Anderson that Miss Edith had asked me to take a book to read to her and had said one that I liked, but I had never read a storybook. I began to look at a case of books. Anderson told me they were all about politics and politicians.

'Come over here' she said, 'there are some novels.'

I picked out two books, *Huckleberry Finn* by Mark Twain, as it had a picture on the front of a grinning boy dressed in rags and *Vanity Fair* by Thakaray because the title seemed interesting. I took them upstairs to Miss Edith who thought that I had made a good choice. There was a stool next to her chair, which she asked me to sit on and read *Vanity Fair* to her. I did this for about half an hour. She asked me if I liked reading to her and if I mind doing it regularly. I said that I had enjoyed it. Miss Ethel said,

'You speak well and your English is good. Were you good at English at school?'

I said that I was and that I was also very fond of poetry. We recited one or two pieces together and she laughed, surprised that she could still remember them. She asked me to wheel her chaise longue to the bathroom door and said that she could manage from there.

A short while later she asked me to go and ask Anderson to make her a small cheese omlette with some thin bread and butter for lunch. I wondered what an omlette was and was intrigued, so I stayed in the kitchen and watched Anderson make it. There were so many things in the house and kitchen that I had never seen before and I meant to learn quickly about their use.

We had our lunch in the kitchen. Anderson had made a dish of cauliflower cheese served with thin bread and butter. I could eat only a small amount and Mrs. Woodward said that I would never grow up if I didn't eat my food. I didn't tell them that I had not tasted cheese before. Anderson then asked Dorothy if she would stay later that afternoon to give Miss Edith her tea, as she and Martin were taking me into town to buy shoes and some other things.

It was a lovely afternoon, the sun was trying to shine, although it was cold. We went first of all to Barrett's shoe shop in Oxford Street. Martin waited outside in the car. When we got inside, Anderson told me to sit on one of the low chairs and take my shoes off. She then went to the assistant and chose me some shoes. After having my feet measured and trying on the shoes, we eventually came away with three pairs, a pair of brown lace-ups for outdoor wear, a pair of black strapped house shoes, and a pretty pair of red bedroom slippers. Anderson gave them to Martin to look after while we walked further down the road to John Lewis's. I was bought a brown tweed coat, a brown velour hat and two more frocks, which were left behind to be delivered later as they needed altering. We then went back to Martin and he came into a shop with us where we all had tea and biscuits. After this Martin said he must take us home quickly as he had to meet Miss Hilda at 5 o'clock in the City.

That evening Miss Hilda took me into the lounge and asked me if I had enjoyed my first day, and whether I thought that I could live there. I told her that I would love to stay at the house, but was still wondering about my duties. I explained that I thought I had to work for everything that I had. She said,

'My dear, my sister and I always wanted to share our house and offer a home to a child, but because neither of us are married we are not able to. It was Anderson who gave us the idea of having somebody to help her with the care of Miss Edith.'

She then said,

'It took Anderson and me a long time to find you and we are both sure that you are just the right person. We all want you to be happy here.'

Then she went on to tell me that she would find out where Eva was so that she could visit me and that she also knew I had an Aunt and Uncle who lived in the Holloway Road. She said that she would supply me with everything that I wanted and would arrange an allowance for me with Anderson. It was also suggested that I went to college for two days a week. (I studied English Literature and maths for one and a half years passing all of the leaving exams.) We sat for quite a while. I don't remember what we talked about, I only know that I enjoyed talking with her. She was naturally friendly and easy to talk to and when she smiled it lit up her whole face, like a ray of sunshine. Later in the evening she kissed me tenderly and said,

'Goodnight, it's time you were off to bed.'

My New Family

For the next few weeks everything went smoothly. Anderson let me have a free hand in what I liked to do. I helped Dorothy with the beds, arranged the flowers from the garden, and answered Miss Edith's bell each time she rang it. Then one morning while I was reading *The Good Companions* to Miss Edith, there was a commotion downstairs. When I opened the door I heard Martin telling the caller that if she did not have an appointment with anyone in the house, then she must come to the back door. I heard a lady answer and immediately I recognised the voice. I nearly went downstairs but Miss Edith called to me to ask what the trouble was. I did not tell her of my suspicions and just explained that a caller had come to the wrong door. She said,

'Come and sit down and read me more about the wanderings of that concert party.'

Later, when I came down to lunch, nothing was said about the caller and I felt relieved as it could not have been who I thought it was.

Two evenings after this I was in bed when Miss Hilda came in to see me. Coming straight to the point she said,

'Your mother has been to see me. She says that she wants you to go and live with her as she is now able to make a home for you.'

I was struck dumb. I did not know what to say. Then, after a little thought, I asked her if Mother could do this. Miss Hilda said she did not know as she didn't have a lot of knowledge about those sorts of things but said,

'I do know that I cannot keep you against your will and she is your mother.'

She talked to me about the law and wondered if Mother *really* had a home, or whether she was living in service. She could not imagine what Mother was up to and thought she must have some plans. I replied that wherever Mother was, or what her plans were, I knew definitely that I did not want to *see* her, let alone live with her. Suddenly I felt very scared and all of my insecurities came back. I said that I did not want to be a nuisance or cause any trouble but begged to stay with them. Miss Hilda said that she knew a Councillor and JP, Mr. Kerr, and she would write to him for an appointment to ask his advice. She then asked me if I had been to see Auntie Ethel lately, and I told her that I had. Miss Hilda then said,

'I think she must have given your mother our address. Why don't you write to her to find out what is going on, or go and see her and invite her here for tea?'

I felt very unhappy and tears swelled up in my eyes. Miss Hilda said in a very matter-of-fact way,

'Don't be a ninny, your world hasn't come to an end, we will get over this little problem.'

She kissed me goodnight, then left me.

For a few days after this I felt down in the dumps. I went to see Auntie Ethel and she admitted that she had told Mother where I lived. She said that she thought Mother probably only wanted to see if I was alright. I invited Auntie Ethel to visit me for tea and she accepted, saying that she would like to see the nice house that I lived in. I asked her if she could bring Eva with her if possible.

It was about a fortnight later when Auntie Ethel, Eva and Mr. Kerr came to tea. The meeting was very cordial but Auntie Ethel and Eva were determined about one thing, that it would not be good for me to go and live with Mother. Mr. Kerr asked me if I wanted to be fostered but I did not know what that meant. He explained that it would mean that Miss Hilda would become my guardian and that she would be responsible for my care and behaviour and that I would become her ward. I said that I did not want to be separated from Eva and Auntie Ethel and asked if I would still be able to visit them. Mr. Kerr and Miss Hilda both assured me that I would be allowed to visit them, and even Mother, if I felt like it.

It was some weeks after this that Martin took Miss Hilda and me in the car to County Hall in Westminster. On the way, we stopped in Holloway Road to pick up Auntie Ethel and Eva. When we arrived at County Hall we were shown up some wide stone steps into a committee room with a long table with leather seated chairs around it. We were there for a few minutes when four smartly dressed men came in.

We all stood up, then were ordered to sit down. Two of the men were Welfare Officers and the other two were Councillors. For some time they talked amongst themselves referring to the notes in front of them. Then one of the Welfare Officers asked me to stand up, asked my name, age and where I had lived until I was fifteen and then asked me if I had seen Mother in that period. He asked Miss Hilda how it was that I came to be in her house. One of the Councillors asked if we knew why Mother was in care at the time I left St. Mary's, but the other Officer said he did not think it was relevant to this case. I was very disappointed at this answer because I did not know why Mother went back in the Workhouse. After this, Miss Hilda, Auntie Ethel and Eva were asked to leave the room and I was left facing the four men. Firstly, they asked me what kind of work I had been doing in Miss Hilda's house and whether the staff were kind to me. Next they asked me how many hours I worked and what my wages were. I answered the questions as best I could and I told them that I did very little work and would be happier if I did more. At this, the gentlemen laughed, I don't think that they understood me really. Next I was asked if I liked Mother. I said that I had no feelings about her, I neither liked nor disliked her and just wished that she would forget all about me. They called the others back into the room and when they were seated, one of the Welfare Officers read out a paper about the aims of the Council regarding illegitimate children. I was a bit confused but then they told Miss Hilda that she would be sent a form with the Council's conditions of fostering which we were both to sign and she would then become my legal guardian.

We were all delighted and to celebrate, on the way home we went to the Army and Navy Stores for tea. I felt so happy I could not get home quick enough to tell Anderson and Miss Edith the good news.

I was the first out of the car and rushed inside the house to tell Miss Edith what had happened. I ran up the stairs and went straight to her room where she was sitting on the sofa with Anderson. Anderson moved aside and patted the space between them for me to sit down and said,

'What was it like? Were they nice to you?'

Before I could answer her, Miss Hilda came up the stairs saying,

'She will not answer any questions until she has taken off her hat and coat, hung them up and changed her shoes.'

I jumped up quickly to obey and met Miss Hilda outside the door. She said quietly,

'I want to talk to Miss Edith for a while, so go down and help Anderson to get the supper on. All four of us will have it upstairs this evening.'

I was unable to express my excitement at supper because Miss Hilda did most of the talking. The three ladies were planning my immediate future. Miss Hilda said that although she had noticed that I liked helping in the house, she did not want me to be given any regular duties. She thought that I should get out more, join a swimming or tennis club or the Society of Friends youth club. Then she turned to me and said,

'Well my dear, what do you think of all this? As Quakers we belong to the Society of Friends which means that all of us here are equal and have responsibilities to one another and I am sure there is something that you would like to do to help in the smooth running of the house.'

Then I realised that all three ladies were looking at me and I wondered what I should say. I was a bit puzzled as I had heard Miss Hilda say that she did not want me to do any regular duties, yet she was asking me to help with the running of the house. After a minute of silence Miss Edith said to me, persuasively,

'Wouldn't you still like to come upstairs and read to me? I would be so grateful, as I enjoy your company and you always do the flowers so nicely for me. And then there are the house plants, Martin will tell you how to look after them.'

I answered, 'Yes', to these suggestions and was very pleased that Miss Edith enjoyed my company, but I thought that I was not asked to do very much. Then Miss Hilda said that she had noticed I did not like attending the meetings on Sunday mornings or mid-week. She told me that I did not have to go although she wanted me to be a member of a church. She felt that, to live in harmony with them, I should be a practising Christian. She asked again if I liked living there and if I was sure that I wanted to stay. I was amazed at such a question and told them I loved it there and I would do my best to fit in. Miss Hilda stopped me and said,

'You do not have to make any promises, just be your natural self. You have brought us a lot of happiness already, we love having you and are all very fond of you.'

She then told me that they would be giving me an allowance of thirty pounds a year to cover my stationary, stamps and other small expenses. She also took me to the bank and taught me how to withdraw money. Miss Hilda told me that she and Miss Edith had agreed that there was no need for me to address them as 'Miss', except when speaking about them to the domestic staff. She reminded me that she would have to fill in the form for the Council about the guardianship which meant that I would be in her care until I was twenty one and that I had to sign the form too. She stated that they had done this because Mother was so possessive and had not actually got a decent home to offer me and they also felt that Mother could be a bad influence. Miss Hilda advised me to stay away from Mother but told me she would write to her from time to time to let her know how I was. She said that I could, of course, keep in touch with Eva and Auntie Ethel.

When I went to bed that night I had a lot to think about. The talk had all sounded very formal and serious but at least I understood my position clearly now. I had also been told that evening that Aunt Hilda (the name I decided to call her) was a journalist, employed by *The Manchester Guardian* as a foreign correspondent. Anderson told me that Aunt Hilda had travelled to many countries; Greece to report on an earthquake, China to write about their terrible floods, most recently to Japan, and she was now planning to go to Russia to study Communism.

As I went to sleep that night I felt more confident and for the first time I felt secure and as if a heavy load had been lifted from me.

Aunt Hilda was often away from home so Aunt Edith and I became great friends, much to the pleasure of Anderson. I enjoyed caring and doing any little thing for her and would always answer her bell myself. Anderson said that Miss Edith was much happier.

For the next two years everything went on smoothly, until April 1935 when Aunt Edith's condition began to deteriorate. She complained of pain more often and was not eating even the daintiest morsels that Anderson offered. Aunt Hilda had her desk taken upstairs so that she could do most of her typing in Aunt Edith's room. The doctor sent in two nurses to look after her, so I was left with very little to do. Aunt Hilda decided that I should go away for a holiday, so she arranged with my sister Eva for me to stay with our relations in Lowestoft. (I did not know until then that I had an aunt and uncle there.) Although I was looking forward to meeting my new relations, I did not want to leave Aunt Edith. I felt that her nurses were *alright* but were very straight laced and staid in their manner. Every morning when I went in to see Aunt Edith, one of them would remind me to be very quiet, and not to stay too long. But Aunt Edith always appeared pleased to see me and would hold my hand to not let me go away and seemed content just to have me sitting beside her. She would give me a naughty grin when she heard the nurse telling me it was time I went and often she would say,

'Come back soon and stay longer', so that the nurse could hear her.

A few days later Dorothy had packed my case and Martin was waiting in the car to take me to Liverpool Street Station. I still had not plucked up enough courage to say goodbye to Aunt Edith. I had a feeling that it was going to be very difficult. I asked Anderson if she would give the nurse her coffee downstairs so that I could be alone with Aunt Edith. I went into her room and she was laying down with her eyes closed, as though she was asleep. When I bent down to kiss her, she looked up at me through a glitter of tears and said in a breathless rush of words, laughing and weeping by runs,

'Oh my dear, I remember when you first came to us, you brought us all so much joy and happiness. You were such a cute little thing. We knew at once that you were the right little girl for us.'

Words failed me. I lifted her up in my arms and kissed her. I was unable to say how much I loved her and what a lot I had to thank *her* for. My tears were falling on her face, mingling with hers and making her very wet. I gently laid her back onto her pillow, got her towel and wiped her face.

The door opened very quietly and Anderson took hold of my arm to draw me away. I kissed Aunt Edith again and said that I would be back when she was better and the nurses had been sent away. When I went to my room to wash and get ready to leave for Lowestoft, I was greatly moved by Aunt Edith's warmth and love. I had an awareness of a flow of good feeling inside me and I realised that for the first time in my life I actually loved someone.

Epilogue

Eva came to see me whilst I was in Lowestoft and told me the sad news that Auntie Edith had died. I inherited £250.00 and since I wanted to do some work it was decided that I use the money to study at Sir Truby King's Mothercraft College. This was a two-year course in the care of babies and children under seven years of age.

In 1939 war was declared and there were many jobs advertised for women in all different types of trades and services. I worked as a clerk in the fireservice from 1939 until 1942. After the war I went to Birmingham Sally Oak Quaker College to study social science but left after one year. Auntie Edith died in 1950 and by this time I had completed two nursing courses and was able to work full time caring for children.

For the whole of my childhood and working life I have cared for children. I think that my background has helped me a lot and I have always enjoyed my work. Now that I have retired I still do voluntary work for Save the Children Fund and for a local old people's club and up until recently I was the treasurer for The National Association for the Welfare of Children in Hospital.

After nearly twenty years of retirement I still get very upset by what I see in the news about the abuse of children. How is it that in these days of enlightenment and education, there are so many children and young people deprived of love? It is for this reason that I wrote the story of my childhood.

Kathleen Dalley 1998

About QueenSpark Books

QueenSpark is a community writing and publishing group based in Brighton. We believe that everyone has a history and that anyone who wants to can be a writer. Our aim is to encourage and publish writing by people who do not normally get into print. QueenSpark Books is not a commercial company. We have two part-time paid workers, but the rest of us are volunteers who work together to write and produce books, gaining and sharing skills and confidence as we go.

We have several active writing workshops in Brighton and Hove. Our manuscripts group reads all manuscripts that are sent to us and sets up book-making groups for those we decide to publish. All groups are run on a co-operative basis.

QueenSpark Books is a member of the national Federation of Worker Writers and Community Publishers. We can give you the addresses of other Federation groups and information on the books they publish.

QueenSpark gratefully acknowledges the support of South East Arts, the local council of Brighton and Hove, and the Foundation for Sport and the Arts.

If you would like more information, or to get involved in any of our activities, please contact:

QueenSpark Books
49 Grand Parade
Brighton BN2 2QA
Telephone and Fax (01273) 571710